DATE DUE

~~APR 8 98~~			

DEMCO 38-296

PRIVATIZATION AND CAPITAL MARKET DEVELOPMENT

PRIVATIZATION AND CAPITAL MARKET DEVELOPMENT

Strategies to Promote Economic Growth

Michael P. McLindon

Foreword by
Ceslav Ciobanu

 PRAEGER

Westport, Connecticut
London

Library of Congress Cataloging-in-Publication Data

McLindon, Michael P.
    Privatization and capital market development : strategies to
promote economic growth / Michael P. McLindon ; foreword by Ceslav
Ciobanu.
        p.   cm.
    Includes bibliographical references and index.
    ISBN 0–275–95066–2 (alk. paper)
    1. Capital market. 2. Privatization. I. Title.
HG4523.M35   1996
332'.0414—dc20   96–21320

British Library Cataloguing in Publication Data is available.

Library of Congress Catalog Card Number: 96–21320
ISBN: 0–275–95066–2

First published in 1996

Praeger Publishers, 88 Post Road West, Westport, CT 06881
An imprint of Greenwood Publishing Group, Inc.

Printed in the United States of America

The paper used in this book complies with the
Permanent Paper Standard issued by the National
Information Standards Organization (Z39.48–1984).

10 9 8 7 6 5 4 3 2

*This book is dedicated to
the memory of my father,
Gerald J. McLindon.*

CONTENTS

TABLES

FOREWORD

By the end of the twentieth century, history has proven that there is no alternative to an economy driven by market forces based on fair competition. After the collapse of the Soviet Union, many of the newly independent states (NIS) have chosen to transform their economies from command to market-based ones. Experience is a convincing argument in favor of private property and free markets.

This is why the topic selected by the author of this book—*Privatization and Capital Market Development: Strategies to Promote Economic Growth*—and the comprehensive analysis of the problems of transforming state property into private property (without a revolution) is timely and significant. In this book, the author makes sound recommendations for countries in transition and other emerging market countries. The author is perfectly right when he suggests that governments should shift their portfolio of economic interventions out of areas of the economy in which the private sector could perform better. Mass privatization of state-owned enterprises (SOEs) can play a key role in this shift, along with concurrent development and strengthening of the capital markets. Healthy and liquid capital markets lower the cost of capital for business and therefore enhance economic growth.

The fate of democratic and economic transformations depends on the political will of governments. A successful example of transformation is the case of Moldova. Moldova is one of the first countries in the NIS to implement an ambitious mass privatization program, which was the centerpiece of its economic reforms. In less than two years, Moldova privatized about 2,000 SOEs, which make up two-thirds of its industrial base; and 3.5 million citizens out of a population of 4.5 million have become shareholders. At the same time, in an effort to develop capital markets, Moldova inaugurated the Chisinau Stock Exchange and created the basic capital market infrastructure. About 95 percent of the shares traded on the stock exchange are the shares of privatized SOEs. Moldova also pursued a tight monetary policy which was in line with the recommendations of Milton Friedman, whom I met personally to discuss the challenges facing our country. The effective introduction of the national currency and maintenance of its stability (in the summer of 1995 the Moldovan Leu was the first currency from the former Soviet Union to be recognized as convertible) has helped cut the budget deficit and reduce inflation from 2,800 percent in 1993 to 24 percent in 1995. These policies stopped the economic decline and created the appropriate framework for development.

The emergence of private companies and stock market infrastructure in Moldova has opened the way to foreign capital inflows into the economy, a key factor for technology transfer, the creation of new jobs, and an increase in the export capacity. Moldova is joining the global economy. This is critical because at the end of the twentieth century we are all neighbors even if we do not have common borders. According to the projections of the World Bank, 1996 will bring Moldova a growth of 6 to 8 percent in GDP. Overall, the program was rated by the experts of the World Bank and the International Monetary Fund as the best program in the NIS and an effective model for other reformers to follow.

In this context, the book authored by Michael McLindon is valuable not only because he has done an admirable job in analyzing the experiences of different countries around the world, but also because he has had a direct contribution in the creation of the market economy in Moldova by participating as project manager in its mass privatization project.

I first met Michael in February 1994 when I served as economic advisor to President Snegur of Moldova. Michael had recently arrived as project manager of a large technical assistance team from Price Waterhouse to assist in implementing Moldova's mass privatization program. The work of this team was graciously funded by the United States Agency for International Development (USAID) as part of its program to help countries of the former Soviet Union make the change to a market economy. A few weeks later, after the general elections, the Ministry of Privatization was created and I was named the Minister of Privatization.

At the Ministry, we have good memories of our work with Michael and his team, whom we made an integral part of our efforts to get the program up and running. We met virtually every day and worked long hours to do what was necessary to make mass privatization work: distributing the vouchers to citizens, establishing an auction network, preparing enterprises quickly and efficiently for privatization, engaging the private sector to manage the collection and processing of bids, and drafting legislation for the program.

The cooperation between the Ministry and Michael and his team was critical to the success of our program. I appreciated his leadership and experience, his skills in negotiating, and his emphasis on finding practical solutions to problems. I would like to thank him for his key contributions during this time. (Thanks are also owed to Walter Coles of USAID for his support of our program and to Price Waterhouse.)

Although word of our success traveled slowly at first, by September 1994 a number of distinguished visitors had come to our central mass privatization auction site in Chisinau and noted with enthusiasm the achievements of our program. These honorable visitors included President

Snegur, Speaker of the Parliament Lucinski, U.S. Senators Patrick Leahy, Henry Brown, and Thad Cochrane, former U.S. Ambassador to Moldova Mary Pendleton (and subsequently the current U.S. Ambassador to Moldova, Todd Stewart), USAID Assistant Administrator Thomas Dine, USAID NIS privatization officer Walter Coles, and senior officials from the World Bank.

Mass privatization is not a method to make all the citizens of a country rich, but it helps to ensure fairness and a chance for everyone to participate in the reform. These transformations are long-term events, and the economic effect does not occur overnight. With time, though, privatization and capital markets development can in fact be a rewarding part of the reform process: Citizens become shareholders, workers get ownership in their firms, new jobs are created, firms have more financing options, and the economy benefits from greater efficiency.

I enthusiastically recommend that my counterparts in other countries, and others involved in economic policy making, consider the ideas presented in this book.

Ceslav Ciobanu, Ph.D.

Minister, Ministry of Privatization,
and professor of economics
Chisinau, Moldova

PREFACE

This book grows out of my experience as an advisor on privatization, capital markets, and economic reforms in a number of countries. I decided to write this book after several years of searching for, but not finding, a comprehensive discussion of the themes it treats: the links between privatization and capital markets, and how they support and reinforce each other to promote economic growth.

My hope is that this book will provide some useful insights for policymakers in developing countries and in the international donor agencies, for academics and practitioners involved in economic development, and for the internationally minded private sector in developing and developed countries alike. Privatization, in its various forms, and the development of capital markets will be a primary catalyst for economic growth and globalization well into the twenty-first century.

I would like to express my keen appreciation to the following people for their review of all or parts of this book: Kathleen Avvakumovits, Sylvie Bossoutrot, Martin Chrisney, Ceslav Ciobanu, Gray Cowan, Paul Elicker, Paul Fratarnico, Matthew Hensley, John Horton, William Joslin, Yohannes Kassahun, Gabriela Koika, Patricia Lerner,

David Levintow, William Mako, Patricia Moser, Richard Pinkham, Rudyard Robinson, Georgia Sambunaris, Richard Samuelson, Nemat Shafik, Asita R. De Silva, Samuel Skogstad, Tommy White, and Ned White. Their comments and suggestions have helped to make this a better book, although the final product does not necessarily reflect their views or those of the company or institution they work with. Any remaining errors, and the substance and conclusions of this book, remain my responsibility.

I have had the privilege and honor of working as an advisor in over twenty countries, and would like to express my appreciation for these opportunities, which have had a decisive impact on the development of the ideas expressed in this book.

Thanks are also due to Matthew Hensley, Tommy White, and Ned White, Group Directors of the Institute for Public–Private Partnerships. The Institute's training workshops have afforded me an opportunity, during the last year, to present some of the ideas contained in this book and to benefit from the ensuing discussions with distinguished participants from many countries.

Michael P. McLindon
Washington, D.C.

ABBREVIATIONS

ADR American Depositary Receipt
BLO Build–Lease–Operate
BO Build–Operate
BOO Build–Own–Operate
BOT Build–Operate–Transfer
BT British Telecom
BTO Build–Transfer–Operate
CFA Chartered Financial Analyst
CSE Colombo Stock Exchange
DFI Development Finance Institution
EGAT Electricity Generating Authority of Thailand
FCC Federal Communications Commission
FELT Fair, Efficient, Liquid, and Transparent
FERC Federal Energy Regulatory Commission
GDP Gross Domestic Product
GNP Gross National Product
IFC International Finance Corporation
IMF International Monetary Fund
IPO Initial Public Offering

KEPCO	Korean Electric Power Corporation
NCB	National Commercial Bank (Jamaica)
NIC	Newly Industrializing Country
NIS	Newly Independent States
OECD	Organization for Economic Co-Operation and Development
ROT	Rehabilitate–Operate–Transfer
SEC	Securities and Exchange Commission
SET	Securities Exchange of Thailand
SOE	State-Owned Enterprise
TOJ	Telecommunications of Jamaica
TOT	Telephone Organization of Thailand
USAID	United States Agency for International Development

All dollar figures are for U.S. dollars unless otherwise indicated.

CHAPTER ONE

INTRODUCTION

Privatization and the development of capital markets aim to correct, with other reforms, decades of flawed development strategies. When implemented as separate policies, privatization and capital markets development each work to promote economic growth. But when governments take advantage of the synergies between the two, efforts at privatization and capital market development are stronger, more effective, and more sustained in promoting growth.

To modernize and industrialize after World War II, governments in developing countries took the lead role in the economy.[1] They intervened by creating state-owned enterprises (SOEs) in leading sectors.[2] They dominated finance by nationalizing banks and establishing development finance institutions (DFIs) to direct capital to SOEs and favored projects. They borrowed heavily from abroad to do both.

The oil shocks of the 1970s created grave problems for many developing countries. The dollars deposited in international banks by oil-exporting countries were lent to oil-importing developing countries to adjust to oil shocks. However, this debt, which financed inefficient SOEs and budget deficits, was not productively invested and did not create the means to repay debt.

In 1982, Mexico precipitated the debt crisis when it announced that it could not service its debt. International finance to developing countries dried up. The world recession of 1981–1982 and decline in export earnings deepened the financial woes of developing countries. These crises hastened the exposure of the defects of intervention: SOEs and domination of finance by government hindered rather than promoted growth.

In the 1980s and 1990s, governments adopted reform measures that have included the privatization of SOEs and the development of private sector capital markets. But, while some developing countries have had success in privatization and capital markets, most have yet to undertake these reforms in earnest.

This introductory chapter discusses the experience with privatization and capital markets over the last decade, and the potential of both to promote economic growth. It then reviews data to show that for most developing countries, neither privatization nor capital markets has firmly taken root. The chapter then presents robust recommendations about the desirability of using privatization by broad-based share sales and mass privatization, Build–Operate–Transfer (BOT) infrastructure privatization, and the privatization of institutional investors such as social security to realize the benefits of privatization and develop capital markets as quickly as possible.

THE POTENTIAL OF PRIVATIZATION AND CAPITAL MARKETS

Privatization and capital market development are key to reform and development: They mitigate the distortions that follow from flawed strategies, and promote economic growth through several different but complementary channels.

Privatization enables a government to shift its portfolio of economic interventions out of areas of the economy in which the private sector can perform better, freeing resources for those areas that are the basic responsibilities of government. Studies have shown that privatization improves the competitiveness and efficiency of enterprises, which promotes economic growth.[3]

Capital markets support economic growth by channeling savings to long-term productive investment on the basis of market signals and prospects for risk and return, rather than government fiat. Empirical studies suggest that capital markets indeed have an important role to play in promoting growth in developing countries. The lack of capital markets, in contrast, hinders the development of the private sector in industry, commerce, and infrastructure. Without a capital market to efficiently channel domestic saving to productive long-term investment, economic growth cannot be sustained.

The most important types of privatization include public share sales, mass privatization by vouchers, the privatization of social security and other potential institutional investors, and BOT privatization for economic infrastructure. (The various types of privatization are defined and discussed in Chapter 2.)

Governments in developed and developing countries have transferred an estimated $438 billion in SOEs to the private sector since 1985, including $80.3 billion in 1994.[4] More than 100 countries have privatization activities of one sort or another underway.[5] As of 1995, about 35,000 medium and large SOEs have been privatized.[6]

Economic reforms, including privatization, have helped capital markets to emerge in some countries. Market capitalization for fifty-nine developing countries soared from $171.2 billion in 1985 to $1.9 trillion in 1994, an elevenfold increase.[7] Some emerging capital markets have come to serve as primary sources of capital for enterprises to finance long-term investment, and thereby promote economic growth.[8] According to the International Finance Corporation (IFC), there have been important improvements in capital markets infrastructure, including clearing and settlements, custodial arrangements, and investor protection in emerging markets, though much remains to be done.

Countries in Western Europe, Latin America, Asia, Eastern Europe and the former Soviet Union illustrate how privatization and capital markets complement each other:

- The United Kingdom, a pioneer in privatization, demonstrated in the 1980s, despite skepticism, that shares of large SOEs could be sold in the stock market, stimulating growth through new shareholders and market trading. Other Western European countries have adopted a similar strategy in the 1990s.

- Building on the models of privatization in the United Kingdom, some emerging market countries in Latin America, such as Chile and Argentina, and in Asia, such as Malaysia and Korea, privatized SOEs through share sales in the late 1980s and 1990s. Their success in selling billions of dollars of shares in SOEs showed how emerging capital markets can be harnessed to support privatization, which further develops capital markets.

- Governments in Latin America and Asia have also been successful in privatizing the provision of economic infrastructure through BOT techniques. These permit the private sector to finance, construct, manage, and own economic infrastructure projects and earn a reasonable profit through user fees and tolls. Some BOT projects have raised hundreds of millions of dollars in local and foreign investment.

- Chile's privatization of its social security system has provided high returns to future pensioners and bolstered its capital markets, which had been rejuvenated by earlier privatization of SOEs.

- The Czech and Slovak Federal Republic, Russia, Lithuania, Moldova, and Kyrgyzstan applied the techniques of mass privatization by vouchers to thousands of enterprises, creating millions of shareholders and hundreds of investment funds, and thus the critical mass for capital markets. The techniques developed are now available to be used in other countries—not just the former command economies—which seek to speed up the privatization process and develop capital markets.

Countries with functioning, even if rudimentary, stock markets can undertake privatizations by share sale of SOEs, encouraging private companies to consider selling shares to outside investors to raise equity finance. Capital markets compete with the banking system, but also complement it. A strong equity market helps to strengthen the balance sheets of companies. Stronger balance sheets facilitate larger loans of longer matur-ities; this, in turn, develops a market for the banks and may enable them to play a capital market role by extending the length of their loans. A stock market makes venture-capital financing feasible for start-up firms: The entrepreneur and venture capitalists can be repaid for their labors and risks endured.

Companies that meet requirements for information in the stock market groom themselves for bond financing, which reduces the cost of capital to firms and further develops capital markets. The informational requirements of a capital market also encourage the development of higher accounting standards.

Economic infrastructure, such as telecommunications, power, transportation, and municipal services, are necessary for economic growth, but too often governments are unable to supply the needed levels of infrastructure. Governments must open the provision of economic infrastructure to the private sector. Mobilizing finance for infrastructure, in turn, requires the development of capital markets.

Privatization of institutional investors, such as pension funds, mutual funds, and insurance companies, allows them to become professional, active capital markets agents and an important source of demand for stocks and bonds. Strong institutional investors encourage private companies to sell shares to the public.

Privatization can attract direct and portfolio foreign investment, which opens the international capital markets to local companies and fosters the globalization of capital markets. Large privatizations in developing countries have included tranches sold to Western investors. Many privatized companies from developing countries are able to access the U.S. capital market through American Depositary Receipts (ADRs).[9] The ability to place large levels of equity from emerging markets has made privatization worth billions of dollars possible. Access to the international capital markets adds additional competition and efficiency to the country's financial system. Privatizing countries are attractive to foreign investors because of the possibilities of appreciation of share price, risk diversification, and a broader range of available securities.

The benefits of the symbiotic development of privatization and capital markets are within reach for the most advanced and the most rudimentary capital markets alike. For example, the French privatization program of 1993 sponsored new, more sophisticated placement techniques to gauge demand from institutional and individual investors for the shares of privatized companies. These techniques, which allowed French capital markets to become more dynamic and sophisticated, are now available to French securities firms to use in selling shares in private companies. In Moldova, where no capital market had previously existed, a successful mass privatization program transferred shares in over a thousand enterprises to 3.5 million citizens out of a population of 4.5 million, and created private sector capital markets agents.

THE PREVALENCE OF SOEs AND LANGUISHING CAPITAL MARKETS

Although there has been spectacular success in a few countries, data indicate that privatization and capital market development are not as widespread as it may seem. How vigorously do governments privatize worldwide? One may infer from case studies and press headlines that privatization runs deep. But does it? A 1995 World Bank study observes that between 1980 and 1993, ninety-five countries that privatized SOEs only privatized three SOEs a year, on average.[10] (These figures do not include mass privatizations or privatizations under $50,000 in value.) Most countries continue to own hundreds, sometime thousands, of SOEs, which are inefficient, absorb scarce resources, contribute to deficits and inflation, and stifle capital markets and economic growth.

To what extent have capital markets in developing countries emerged? A closer look at the growth of stock market capitalization to $1.9 trillion in 1994 reveals that eight of the fifty-nine countries account for 80 percent of this market capitalization. There are more than one hundred countries beyond these fifty-nine countries that have no capital markets to speak of.

Too often, governments do not understand private sector capital markets and even try to suppress them: The stock market is considered a "casino" which wastes resources or a rival to government domination of finance. Government channeling of capital to SOEs and favored projects, this view holds, is the best way to promote development. In short, privatization and capital market development are far less widespread and less well-understood than commonly believed.

OBJECTIVES AND ORGANIZATION OF THIS BOOK

Much of the literature on privatization falls into one of two categories. The first presents case studies of countries or specific transactions. The second deals with a range of important privatization topics: the reasons for and benefits of privatization; the impact of privatization on the budget, employment, productivity, efficiency, and income distribution; its relationship to other parts of reform; strategies and techniques for privatization; obstacles to implementation; and a range of legal, marketing, valuation, and social issues. These topics have been addressed at length in other works, and generally are not discussed in detail in this book, except occasionally in summary form for the reader's convenience and where relevant to the theme of the interaction of privatization and capital market development.

The literature on capital markets in developed countries is well established. Yet, until the 1980s, the role of capital markets in developing countries was ignored by most policymakers and development economists. The International Finance Corporation, and particularly van

Agtmael, Gill, and Sudweeks, have brought the importance of developing capital markets to the attention of governments, donors, the academic community, and the private sector.

This book accepts as a given (based on a number of previous studies) that privatization, when properly structured and implemented, is beneficial. It highlights techniques of privatization that not only realize the benefits of privatization, but also encourage capital market development, allowing both processes to promote economic growth. It presents evidence that the best methods of privatization are also the best ways to develop capital markets.

This book is based upon the author's experience as an advisor on privatization, capital markets, and economic reform in a number of developing countries in the former Soviet Union, Eastern Europe, Asia, Latin America, and Africa. It also draws on distinguished secondary works to discuss and analyze further the salient points on the interaction between privatization and capital markets.

These facts, analyses, and arguments lead to strong conclusions: Renewed, aggressive approaches are needed to privatize and develop capital markets. Broad-based public share sales have proven to be advantageous as a technique of privatization and a means of developing capital markets. They can be used for a handful of blue-chip SOEs to raise revenue and demonstrate professional techniques of initial public offerings.

At the same time, governments must consider adopting the mass privatization techniques developed in Eastern Europe and the former Soviet Union to quickly privatize remaining SOEs, create large numbers of new shareholders and investment funds, and develop capital markets.

Chapters 2 and 3 set the foundation to develop this theme with discussions of privatization and capital markets, respectively. Chapter 2 identifies problems with SOEs that gave rise to the need for privatization. It summarizes the main types of privatization that are available to governments. It then surveys current trends in economic reform and privatization in the United States, Western

Europe, Latin America, Asia, Africa, Eastern Europe and the former Soviet Union. The findings of a recent World Bank study on the ongoing dominance of SOEs in most developing countries are presented.

Chapter 3 defines basic financial terms and explains the role of financial markets and capital markets in the economy. It then examines the three main reasons why capital markets are underdeveloped: the impact of government policy and practice, the dominance of the banking system in developing countries, and the failure to fully privatize the economy. It summarizes the benefits of capital markets.

Chapter 4 discusses the elements of capital market development (and relates them to privatization), including public awareness, regulation, and development of stock market infrastructure. A general strategy for utilizing privatization to develop a supply of and demand for shares is discussed.

These chapters set the stage for a discussion, in Chapters 5 and 6, of privatization by broad-based share sales and mass privatization. Chapter 5 discusses the experiences of countries in Western Europe, Latin American, and Asia in privatization and capital market development. It discusses the strategy of privatization by broad-based share sale, and its usefulness as a means of developing capital markets.

Chapter 6 discusses why it was necessary to develop a strategy of mass privatization for countries in Eastern Europe and the former Soviet Union. It discusses how privatization is possible without capital markets, and how it plays a key role in building capital markets.

Chapter 7 discusses important areas of growth for privatization and capital market development which will be essential to sustain growth in the future: economic infrastructure (especially telecommunications and power), and institutional investors (such as insurance companies, pension funds, and mutual funds).

Finally, Chapter 8 presents the main conclusions of the book.

At least two limitations to this book can be stated. In trying to provide relevant country experiences, the author has relied primarily, though not exclusively, on those country cases in which he has had direct advisory experience. Efforts have been made to update the situations discussed, although this has not always been possible.

Second, even while its discussion is largely limited to the interaction between privatization and capital markets, this book does not attempt to be exhaustive. An example of one issue that is not covered is the privatization of the provision of land, housing, and housing finance, which governments dominate in many countries, and whose privatization is important for capital market development and economic growth.

Privatization is linked not only to financial capital, but also to human capital. For example, privatization of state schools using vouchers and contracting out is being tried in some countries, including the United States, as a way to reverse the decline in the quality of education. Introducing privatization techniques into education offers the potential to increase and improve human capital, which is the most important factor in a country's long-term growth and development.The importance of these two areas to the overall theme of privatization and capital market development is noted, but a full discussion of them is beyond the scope of this book.

NOTES

1. The term "developing country," as used in this book, follows the World Bank's definition of a country where Gross National Product (GNP) per capita is $8,625 per annum in 1993 or less, including low income ($695 or less), lower-middle income ($696 to $2,785), and upper-middle income economies ($2,786 to $8,625). The term "transitional economy," or "former command economy," is used to describe the countries of Eastern Europe and the former Soviet Union that are currently in the process of transition from a socialist command economy to a market economy. The terms "emerging stock markets," "emerging equity markets," and "emerging market country," as used in this

book, follow the usage by the International Finance Corporation of referring to any market in a developing econ-omy, as defined by the World Bank. As the IFC notes, this implies that these emerging markets have the potential for development, even if they do not have a stock exchange. In fact, for 1995, the IFC's Emerging Stock Markets Factbook had data on only fifty-nine developing countries out of a total of 170 developing countries. See the World Bank's *World Development Report 1995* and the IFC's *Emerging Stock Markets Factbook 1995* for data and further discussion.

2. The World Bank has defined a SOE as a government-owned or government-controlled economic entity that generates the bulk of its revenues from selling goods and services. This definition, the Bank notes, excludes much state-owned activity, such as education, health services, and road construction and maintenance. See World Bank, *Bureaucrats in Business* (New York: Oxford University Press, 1995), 26.

3. See, for example, Ahmed Galal and Mary Shirley, eds., *Does Privatization Deliver? Highlights from a World Bank Conference* (Washington, D.C.: World Bank, 1994); and William L. Megginson, Robert C. Nash, and Matthias van Randenborgh, "The Privatization Dividend: A Worldwide Analysis of the Financial and Operating Performance of Newly Privatized Firms," *Public Policy for the Private Sector,* The World Bank Group, December 1995, 33–36. Some of the results of these studies are discussed in Chapter 2.

4. Fin Mark Research, cited in Reason Foundation, *Privatization 1995* (Los Angeles, Calif.: The Reason Foundation,1995) p. 10. It is important to note that data on privatization, through no fault of the organizations that attempt to gather this information, are, in general, less precise than that for stock markets. Data on privatization vary widely depending on the source, although the trends they capture are usually consistent. Some of the problems with privatization data include the lack of a central "clearing house" for data in any particular country (which is one function that a stock exchange provides), and the different types of privatization that exist. Sources of data on privatizations cited in this book include the various publications of the World Bank, Privatisation International and its *Privatisation Yearbook 1995,* the Reason Foundation, the Cato Institute, the Organization for Economic Co-operation and Development (OECD), and other sources as cited in the text and the Bibliography.

of privatization and presents an overview of privatization trends in different regions of the world. Finally, it discusses the benefits of privatization.

WHY SOEs PERFORM POORLY

SOEs have a tendency to be inefficient and unproductive, thereby restricting economic growth.[3] Most SOEs are units of the government, without a legal corporate status, budgets, accounts, auditors, board of directors, or much sense of managerial and performance accountability. Thus, most elements of effective "corporate governance" are missing, even though SOEs purportedly serve the public interest.

Managers of SOEs often owe their position to patronage rather than competence. Employment policy, in practice, is one of "jobs for the boys," resulting in over-staffing and under-performance, as Tables 2.1 and 2.2 illustrate for the telecommunications sector. Political pressure often results in setting prices of goods and services below their true costs, especially in the utility sectors, such as gas, electricity, and water. As a result, required maintenance and new investment suffer, service to customers deteriorates, and economic growth is impaired.

There is often a lack of true financial accountability. SOEs seldom face hard budget constraints. If faced with losses, many SOEs are successful in lobbying government for subsidies, often their only real source of competitive advantage. In the private sector, managers who do not provide an acceptable rate of return for shareholders are fired, or there is a corporate takeover. In the public sector, this rarely happens. Given the contradictory objectives which SOEs usually face, it is not surprising that performance is poor and incentives for efficient operations are lacking.

TYPES OF PRIVATIZATION

The term "privatization" in this book is used in its broadest sense. E. S. Savas has defined privatization as "the act

Table 2.1
Performance Indicators for Telecommunications Sector: PTT Employees per 1,000 DELs*

	Employees/ 1,000 DELs
Tanzania	69.00
Ecuador	18.00
Hungary	23.00
Indonesia	50.00
Malaysia	50.00
India	96.00
New England Telephone (USA)	0.21
Telefonica (Spain)	0.14
New York Telephone (USA)	0.20
NTT	0.16

Source: William W. Ambrose, Paul R. Hennemeyer, and Jean-Paul Chapon. "Privatizing Telecommunications Systems." IFC discussion paper no. 10, Washington, D.C. The World Bank, 1990.

*Direct Exchange Line: telephone line which connects subscriber to local telephone exchange.

of reducing the role of government, or increasing the role of the private sector, in an activity or in the ownership of assets."[4]

Governments pursuing privatization can choose from a menu of options. Different types of privatization are often used in combination. For example, some governments have sold large stakes in an SOE to a local or foreign investor which will manage and control the company and bring in new capital, technology, and market access. Smaller percentages of the shares are offered to employees and managers, and the public may also be offered shares in a public share offer or as part of a mass privatization program. The basic types of privatization are discussed in the following section.

Table 2.2
Performance Indicators for Telecommunications Sector: 1988 Telephone
Waiting Lists

Market	Wait Period (years)
Algeria	8.5
Argentina	21.9
Colombia	4.3
Egypt	27.1
Ghana	30.0
Indonesia	7.8
Jamaica	22.3
Malaysia	0.6
Pakistan	10.0
Philippines	7.1
Poland	12.2
Sri Lanka	8.5
Tanzania	10.9
Thailand	3.6
Tunisia	5.0
Uruguay	2.8
Venezuela	8.1
Zimbabwe	5.3

Source: William W. Ambrose, Paul R. Hennemeyer, and Jean-Paul Chapon. "Privatizing Telecommunications Systems." IFC discussion paper no. 10, Washington, D.C. The World Bank, 1990.

Liquidation

One privatization measure is simply to liquidate some SOEs. This may be warranted in cases where no combination of new investment, ownership, and operational changes exists which would give the enterprise a positive net present value in terms of future cash flows. Occasionally, the situation of SOEs is so bad that they are simply abandoned without a formal liquidation.

In the former command economies, grave distortions in market signals make it virtually impossible to determine which SOEs can survive and which cannot. For this reason, most SOEs are included in the mass privatization program to transfer them to the private sector, which can determine their survivability better than the bureaucracy which got them into trouble in the first place. Thus, governments can avoid the need to decide which enterprises should be closed and leave this decision to market forces.

Contracting Out

A number of services, including management, can be contracted out to the private sector, usually through a competitive bidding process followed by negotiations. Contracting out is a useful technique for some services, such as garbage collection and disposal, urban bus services, and prison management.

Some countries have also used contracting out for the management of SOEs. For example, governments frequently use management contracts for hotels. Contracting out services usually leads to an improvement in day-to-day operations. However, contracting out does not address the need for new investment in plant, equipment, and technology to keep the enterprise competitive. Another drawback is that contracting out does not transfer ownership to the private sector, which is critical for sustained improvement in enterprise performance.

Leasing

A lease enables a private sector group to control a company or assets or both, for a period of time, for financial gain. Leasing is a more powerful tool than contracting out, since the returns to the lessee are more directly determined by the lessee's success in managing the leased assets. As with contracting out, however, the problem of making new investment in the enterprise, and the problem of ownership, remain. In the former Soviet Union, leasing occasionally has been used as a device to avoid the stronger forms of privatization, such as mass privatization.

Deregulation and Demonopolization

Under this form of privatization, the government removes regulations which had previously prevented the private sector from competing with a state-owned monopoly, or changes old regulations or creates new ones to foster greater competition from the private sector. In some countries, deregulation has allowed the private sector to offer banking, insurance, mutual fund, and pension fund management services, which are critical to developing capital markets, but too often moribund under government monopoly control.

Management–Employee Buyouts

Occasionally, management or employees or both may be ideal buyers for an SOE, especially for smaller enterprises. This is especially so when management is otherwise effective but performance has been compromised by ministerial directives and other operational constraints.

In the former Soviet Union, managers and employees had the option of buying large controlling blocks in enterprises at very favorable prices. This method may have made post-privatization restructuring more difficult, but was judged to be necessary to secure support from managers and employees who otherwise could have delayed the privatization process.

Trade Sales

A trade sale involves the sale of controlling interests in an enterprise to the private sector, usually through competitive tendering techniques, an evaluation of proposals, and negotiation between the government and the potential private sector buyer. There are three basic types of trade sales. The first two are used for medium- and large-scale enterprises. In a "commercial tender," the decision to award is based on the offer price alone. In an "investment tender," price and other factors, such as new investment and job retention, are taken into consideration in the evaluation. The third method, the open-outcry auction, is frequently used for small enterprises.

Usually, the best practice is to make the award on the basis of price alone. Allowing too much discretion to the evaluators may reduce the appearance of transparency and discredit the process. A disadvantage of trade sales is that they may effectively limit participation in privatization to wealthy local investors or foreign investors. This could discredit the overall process of economic reform if the poor and middle class feel that the burden of adjustment falls on them while others gain, possibly unfairly. The use of trade sales alone may limit the impact of privatization on developing capital markets, in comparison with other forms of privatization which enable more people to participate.

Public Share Sales

Public share sales can overcome the potential problems of trade sales by virtue of their greater transparency and openness to the public. Properly structured, marketed, and priced, "broad-based" public share sales can help to popularize the privatization program, spread the benefits of economic reform and ownership, and develop capital markets (see Chapter 5).

Public share sales have been the most salient form of privatization in the 1980s and 1990s. The twenty largest privatizations by share sales between 1984 and 1994 in both developed and developing countries are listed in Table 2.3.

Mass Privatization

The staggering problems encountered by the command economies of Eastern Europe and the former Soviet Union have given rise to a new and rapid approach: mass privatization, which enables countries to privatize thousands of enterprises, utilizing standard techniques, transparent procedures, and vouchers distributed to citizens.

Table 2.3
Top Twenty Privatizations by Public Share Sale (1984–1994)

Country	Privatization	Percentage Sold	Price (US$ millions)
Japan	Nippon Telegraph & Telephone (NTT)	35	70,500
United Kingdom	British Telecom	100	22,800
United Kingdom	British Gas	100	7,600
France	Elf Aquitaine	38	6,200
Mexico	Telefonos de Mexico (Telmex)	100	5,590
Germany	Voag	100	5,144
Netherlands	Koninklijke PTT Nederland	50	3,900
Singapore	Singapore Telecom	11	3,800
United Kingdom	Scottish Power	100	3,665
Argentina	Telecom Argentina (Entel North)	100	3,200
Argentina	Yacimientos Petroliferos Fiscales (YPF)	46	3,000
Argentina	Telefonica de Argentina (Entel South)	100	3,000
Denmark	TeleDanmark	49	3,000
New Zealand	Telecom Corp. of New Zealand	100	2,510
United Kingdom	British Airports Authority	100	2,500
Malaysia	Syarikat Telekom Malaysia Bhd.	27	2,350
United Kingdom	National Power	100	2,278
Spain	Repsol	80	2,215
South Korea	Korea Electric Power Corp. (KEPCO)	21	2,100
Peru	Compania Peruana de Telefonos (CPT) and Entel (Peru)	100	2,002

Source: "The Emerging Infrastructure Industry," a report prepared by the Private Participation in Infrastructure Group, World Bank, Washington, D.C., 1995

Mass privatization through vouchers has expanded the envelope of privatization techniques and strategies, and proven beyond a doubt that substantial privatization can take place even in the absence of capital markets, adequate accounting standards, and legal and other infrastructure—all of which were formerly considered prerequisites to privatization. In fact, mass privatization, when properly structured, can serve as a catalyst for the development of capital markets where none previously existed, although complementary measures (discussed in Chapter 4) are needed to safeguard the gains from mass privatization.

The Czech and Slovak Federal Republic, Russia, Lithuania, Moldova, and Kyrgyzstan are examples of countries which have initiated successful mass privatization programs with vouchers and simultaneously initiated capital markets. These experiences are discussed further in Chapter 6.

Build–Operate–Transfer
Infrastructure Privatization

As important as it is to privatize existing SOEs, the privatization of economic infrastructure, not yet constructed but urgently needed, is just as important. The BOT model (discussed more fully in Chapter 7) is a method of privatization well-suited for addressing infrastructure needs.

This type of privatization involves economic infrastructure (e.g., power, roads, bridges, ports, airports, municipal services) which would be desirable to construct, but cannot be built owing to budgetary limitations. Using BOT and related techniques, the government tenders these projects to the private sector, which assumes responsibility for the financing, construction, and operation of the infrastructure project. Table 2.4 lists the most significant current BOT projects.

BOT infrastructure privatization, which is becoming more prominent in both developed and developing countries, will draw on capital markets for finance, and in turn will spur significant capital market development.

Table 2.4
Top New Private Infrastructure Investment Projects (1984–September 1995)

Location	Project	Contract	Cost (US$ millions)
France/United Kingdom	Channel Tunnel	BOT, 55 years	19,000
Taiwan (China)	Taipei mass rapid transit system	BOT	17,000
Japan	Kansai International Airport	BOT	15,000
Argentina	Buenos Aires water and sewer services	ROT, 30 years	4,000
Thailand	TelecomAsia communications network	BTO, 25 years	4,000
China	Daya Bay nuclear power plant, phase 1	BOO	3,700
Malaysia	North–South toll expressway	BOT, 30 years	3,400
Mexico	Petacalco coal-fired power plant	BOT	3,000
Thailand	Bangkok Elevated Road and Train System	BOT, 30 years	2,981

Source: "The Private Infrastructure Industry—A Global Market of US$60 Billion a Year," a report prepared by the Private Sector Development Department, World Bank, Washington, D.C., 1995.

Notes: BOO = Build–Own–Operate; BOT = Build–Operate–Transfer; BTO = Build–Transfer–Operate; ROT = Rehabilitate–Operate–Transfer.

WORLD TRENDS IN PRIVATIZATION
AND ECONOMIC REFORM

There is growing worldwide interest in reforms to limit government spending, reduce taxes which discourage investment and employment, cut subsidies, remove barriers to trade and investment, eliminate distortions, develop capital markets, and privatize. This section summarizes recent world privatization trends; Chapters 5 and 6 provide more detailed information on individual country experiences.

The United States

The United States presents the impression that it does not need to privatize: The private sector is dominant. Yet scope remains for the world's leading economy to become more efficient and reduce the government's portfolio of interventions.

In the 1970s and 1980s, for example, the United States deregulated the airline, trucking, railroad, telecommunications, and natural gas sectors. Government regulation gave way to private sector competition. The gains to the U.S. economy from these deregulatory measures are an estimated $40 billion per year.[5]

Unlike most countries, the United States has relatively few SOEs, but state and municipal governments are reluctant to let go of those they have. The Reason Foundation estimates that state and local governments have $226.8 billion in state assets which could be sold to the private sector, as Table 2.5 illustrates.

At the federal level, the Cato Institute notes, government owns about one-third of all land in the United States, of which only a "tiny fraction are of environmental or historical significance."[6] It estimates that the market value of oil lands alone is roughly $450 billion. The federal government also owns tens of billions of dollars of mineral stockpiles, buildings, and other assets. The Cato Institute recommends privatizing $20 billion of assets per year over the next ten years, and using the proceeds to help reduce the deficit and retire the national debt.

Table 2.5
Salable State and Municipal Enterprises in the United States

Enterprise Type	Estimated Number	Estimated Market Value (US$ billions)
Airports (Commercial)	87	29.0
Electric Utilities	2,010	16.7
Gas Utilities	800	2.0
Highways and Bridges	N/A	95.0
Parking Structures	37,500	6.6
Ports	45	11.4
Turnpikes	8	7.4
Water Systems	34,461	23.9
Wastewater Facilities	15,300	30.8
Waste-to-Energy Plants	77	4.0
Total		**226.8**

Source: Reason Foundation, *Privatization 1995* (Los Angele, Calif.: The Reason
Foundation, 1995).

   Privatization is gaining favor as federal, state, and local
governments face budget crises and taxpayer dissatisfac-
tion. Recent years have seen an increase in competitive
contracting to the private sector of municipal and state
services, including garbage collection and disposal and
prison management.[7]
   The provision of economic infrastructure, such as roads,
highways, ports, and airports, is one area that the state and
local governments still dominate, although much of this
infrastructure could easily be provided by the private sector once the appropriate legal framework is in place. The
Dulles Greenway, a fourteen-mile expressway in Virginia
built and financed by the private sector, is an innovative
experiment to permit the private sector to provide infrastructure on a BOT basis in return for a reasonable rate
of return on investment. This project could provide a model
for a much-needed expansion of private sector participation in the United States's economic infrastructure.

The project was unsolicited, and came to fruition because of the perseverance of the project sponsors. Throughout the United States, state and local governments have the opportunity to formalize the process of tendering projects and solicit proposals from a range of qualified private sector firms to provide and finance economic infrastructure. This process relieves governments of fiscal burdens and provides needed services to their citizens.

Privatization options for new sectors, such as social security and education, are receiving consideration in view of chronic poor performance by government and limits on budgets. The decision to privatize social security and permit individuals to manage their own retirement accounts would give a tremendous boost to the U.S. capital markets, which are already the world's most sophisticated. This policy would shift the current "pay-as-you-go" system to an individual, privately managed, defined contribution basis. The huge new pools of investment funds would be a spur to additional investment and enable companies to develop new products, services, and technology and bring them to market—and enable other companies to provide needed infrastructure—once this too is opened up to the private sector. A significant percentage of this money would be invested by professional fund managers in emerging markets, stimulating their development. At the same time, such a system of privately managed retirement accounts would provide better, diversified returns for future U.S. pensioners than the current unfunded system does.

Efforts in the United States to halt declining educational performance at the kindergarten through high school levels have spawned efforts at voucher systems, charter schools, and contracts with private sector groups to manage schools, and to provide healthy competition among schools and choice for parents.

Western Europe

In the United Kingdom and other Western European countries, government ownership of industry and commerce began during the Great Depression of the 1920s

and 1930s and expanded after World War II.[8] Western
European governments used four main reasons to create
SOEs, which later found favor in developing countries:

• "Natural monopolies," especially in the utilities sector, appeared to justify state regulation. The best form of regulation, the
  corollary went, would be direct ownership of industry by
  government.
• National security, not only for the defense industry but also
  in other "strategic" sectors, required and justified government ownership.
• Troubled and failing industries had to be rescued to protect
  jobs and income.
• Profitable enterprises provided revenue for government.
  This could be used to cross-subsidize other desirable social
  objectives.

Another tacit but obvious reason for state ownership
was that it was a source of patronage for the government
and politicians in the form of boards on which to serve
and jobs for supporters.

Views on government ownership of industry and commerce changed in the 1980s. Western Europe, suffering
from sluggish growth and a failure to generate new employment, realized that it had to shift more economic
activities to the private sector. Governments decided to
emphasize a smaller number of activities, leaving the
greater part of work and exchange to the private sector.

Other reasons motivate Western European governments
to privatize. Increasingly, they understand the importance
of capital markets, broad-based share ownership, and professional institutional investors to encourage saving and
channel it to productive investment. Western European
governments' confidence in capital markets to play a role
in privatization, and for privatization to spur the growth
of capital markets, grew from the experience of the
United Kingdom and France in the 1980s (discussed in
Chapter 5). In those countries, privatization by share sale
strengthened equity markets through higher market
capitalization and greater liquidity.

In 1994, privatization proceeds in Western Europe were $51 billion. The OECD has estimated that privatization proceeds over the next five years could reach $200 billion.[9]

Other Regions

Most countries in other parts of the world have pursued a development strategy in which the SOEs played a leading role, and have experienced poor results. A recent World Bank study finds that in many developing countries with large SOE sectors, "the inefficiency of the state-owned firms, combined with the attendant state enterprise sector deficits, are hindering economic growth, and making it more difficult for people to lift themselves out of poverty."[10] It finds that the financing of SOEs is a burden on government finances and developing-country banking systems, and may undermine fiscal stability and fuel inflation.

Latin America With the collapse of international trade that followed the depressions of the early 1930s, many Latin American governments began to shift trade strategies away from export-led models dominated by primary products in favor of policies intended to develop local industry.

By the 1950s, governments had assumed a major economic role that drew heavily on the state-led development models employed by some Western European countries twenty years earlier. Latin America added to this model the strategy of import substitution to stimulate industrialization through SOEs. The premise was that infant industries could develop behind tariff protection. Monopoly status was often added to increase protection in the home country.

Sheltered from domestic and international competition, these infant industries never grew up to be efficient, competitive enterprises. They provided a few well-paying jobs for those with the proper connections, while foisting costly, inferior goods and services on the local economy. Latin American SOEs, a World Bank study shows, "turned out to be grossly inefficient, which increased costs, especially in the provision of infrastructure services."[11]

The impact of SOEs went beyond shoddy products. In Latin America, the 1980s have been described as the "lost decade," owing to the debt crisis. Wasteful, inefficient SOEs incurred huge foreign debts in the 1970s and early 1980s. In Argentina, for example, federal SOEs had acquired over $11 billion in foreign debt at the end of 1988.[12] The premise of this lending was that companies could go bankrupt but governments could not. However, SOEs, not government, had to generate the cash flow to repay debt. The poor performance of SOEs did not generate cash; rather, SOEs absorbed cash from the national budget to cover their losses.

From the abyss of the 1980s, many Latin American countries have emerged in the late 1980s and 1990s as leaders in economic reform (as discussed in Chapter 5). They have succeeded in controlling inflation, reducing debt, rolling back import substitution regimes, reducing bureaucracy, privatizing, and developing capital markets. Indeed, Latin America has become the leader in privatization in developing countries. From 1988 to 1993, according to one source, there were 561 privatization transactions in Latin America, valued at $55.1 billion, or 57 percent of the total privatization transaction value in developing countries.[13]

Asia In Asia, especially East Asia, strategies have proven to be much more favorable for development than in Latin America, Africa, and Eastern Europe and the former Soviet Union. Many countries pursued sound policies and maintained the competitiveness of their exports. Still, until recent reforms, the governments created SOEs and dominated finance to the detriment of capital markets. Today, these governments are working to retain the positive elements of their development strategies while privatizing SOEs and economic infrastructure, and developing capital markets, in order to sustain and promote growth.

A World Bank study of Japan, Hong Kong, Korea, Singapore, Taiwan, Indonesia, Malaysia, and Thailand stresses that the remarkable growth rates in these countries from 1965 to 1990 were due to a stable macroeconomy with limited fiscal deficits, moderate inflation, and competitive exchange rates; stable and secure financial systems whose positive interest rates encouraged financial savings; high rates of investment in physical and human capital; policies to promote exports; limited price distortions; and openness to foreign technology.[14]

Until the late 1980s, the financial sectors of many Asian countries were dominated by the banks; by directing credits to industry and subsidizing interest rates, the banks served as handmaidens to industrial policy. However, Asian governments have become skeptical of industrial policy and realize that in a complex international economy, market forces are more efficient than bureaucracy in allocating capital. The World Bank study notes that, popular perceptions notwithstanding, industrial policy was generally not successful in the eight East Asian countries.[15]

Today, governments realize that privatization of SOEs and economic infrastructure is needed to maintain global competitiveness. Korea, for example, whose drive to promote heavy and chemical industries in the 1970s misjudged markets and led to macroeconomic instability, realizes the limits of industrial policy and has taken measures to liberalize its financial system, develop capital markets, and privatize. (The case of Korea is discussed further in Chapter 5.)

Privatizations to raise revenue, provide greater access to private sector capital, and improve enterprise efficiency are the key to greater financial liberalization in Asia. Developing countries in Asia ranked second after Latin America in terms of value of privatization transactions during 1988 to 1993. Between 1988 and 1993, there were 367 privatization transactions in the developing countries of Asia, with a value of $19.7 billion, or 21 percent of the total privatization transactions value in developing countries.[16]

Africa While there are potential success stories in the making, an overview of the continent suggests that although the winds of change sweeping the world and challenging the commanding heights of statism have visited

Africa, they need to do so in a more sustained way. Some of the poorest countries in the world are found in sub-Saharan Africa, which is home to some of the most inefficient and highest concentrations of SOEs.[17] The domination by SOEs has had serious consequences for economic growth, especially in sub-Saharan Africa, where most countries' economies have stagnated or declined since the 1960s.

A recent World Bank report on sub-Saharan Africa notes that no "country has achieved a sound macroeconomic policy stance—which in broad terms means inflation under 10 percent, a very low budget deficit, and a competitive exchange rate." It further notes that there has been no significant reduction in financial flows to SOEs or improvement in their efficiency. SOEs absorb a large share of bank lending, which crowds out the private sector.[18] Between 1988 and 1993, there were 254 privatization transactions in Africa. However, they generated only $3.2 billion in transaction value, or 3 percent of the worldwide value for developing countries.[19]

Eastern Europe and the Former Soviet Union The command economies eschewed the role of market forces and prices of goods and services in the economy. SOEs dominated most of the economy, although the role of SOE management was poorly defined. The financial system was grossly underdeveloped: banks served as conduits and bookkeepers for the decisions of centralized planning, known in the former Soviet Union as *Gosplan*.

In 1989, the command economies of Eastern Europe, and, in 1991, those of the former Soviet Union, in which bureaucrats made almost all decisions, collapsed under the weight of their own inefficiency, incompetence, and corruption. Privatization was the first step in turning these economies around. Many of these countries realized that case-by-case transactions alone would not be sufficient to deal with the thousands of state-owned enterprises which had languished for decades under the mismanagement of command economies. Bold, innovative approaches were therefore needed to privatize

SOEs. Small-scale privatizations of stores and retail establishments were critical to establishing in people's minds that privatization and a market economy can lead to a better quality of life. For medium- and large-scale enterprises, it was necessary to develop mass privatization through vouchers (see Chapter 6).

PRIVATIZATION: HOW WIDESPREAD?

A 1995 World Bank study observes that although the number of privatization transactions has grown, it remains small relative to the stock of SOEs. Table 2.6, based on this study, indicates the number of privatizations in developing countries for the period of 1980 to 1993 and the value of privatizations for the period of 1988 to 1993. From 1980 to 1987, there were 456 privatization transactions. (Values of these transactions are not available.) These privatizations involved primarily small state-owned enterprises in agribusiness, services, and light manufacturing.

Table 2.6
Privatization in Developing Countries (1980–1993)

	1980–1987	1988–1993	
Region	Number of transactions	Number of transactions	Value of transactions (US$ billions)
Africa	210	254	3.2
Asia	108	367	19.7
Latin America	136	561	55.1
Eastern Europe and Central Asia	2	1,097	17.9
Total developing	456	2,279	**96.0**
Developed countries	240	376	174.9
Privatizations worldwide	696	2,655	270.9

Source: World Bank, *Bureaucrats in Business* (New York: Oxford University Press, 1995).

From 1988 to 1993, there were 2,279 privatizations (these figures do not include mass privatizations or privatization transactions under $50,000 in value). The value of these transactions is estimated at $96 billion. Governments privatized large SOEs in electric and water utilities, transportation, telecommunications, and major firms in the financial and industrial sectors. In developed countries, there were 240 transactions between 1980 and 1987; there were 376 transactions between 1988 and 1993, with a value of $174.9 billion.[20]

The study observes that between 1980 and 1993, ninety-five countries that privatized SOEs only privatized three SOEs a year, on average. (Again, these figures do not include mass privatizations or privatization under $50,000 in value.) This figure is to be compared with the hundreds of SOEs which most countries continue to own. The study notes that SOE value-added as a percentage of developing-country GDP has not decreased over time, nor has the share of SOE employment as a percent of total employment.[21]

BENEFITS OF PRIVATIZATION

The fact that many governments retain large numbers of SOEs indicates that an understanding of the benefits of privatization may be lacking. What are the benefits of privatization?

Greater Efficiency and Productivity of Enterprises

It has been argued that the main benefits of privatization would come from the greater efficiency and productivity of enterprises after privatization. Freed from government control with its set of incompatible objectives (as discussed in the beginning of this chapter), privatized enterprises can focus on being competitive to produce, at low cost and acceptable quality, the goods and services which consumers want. This would lead to a more efficient use of resources and improve economic output overall.

What does the empirical evidence indicate about these benefits of privatization? The World Bank and Boston University analyzed twelve cases of privatization of SOEs in four countries. The team described their findings as "striking. . . . In eleven of twelve cases, the gains were positive and large, amounting to an average 2.5 percent permanent increase in GDP." Beneficial changes that followed privatization included an increase in investment, a rise in prices toward levels that reflect scarcity values, greater productivity thanks to managerial effort, better marketing and diversification, and freedom to shed excess labor.[22]

A broader study by Megginson, Nash, and van Randenborgh compared the pre- and post-privatization performance of sixty-one companies in thirty-two industries in six developing and twelve developed countries. The study indicated that there were significant increases among newly private firms in profitability, output per employee, capital spending, and employment.[23]

Profitability, as measured by return on sales, increased, on average, by 45 percent after privatization. Efficiency was measured by inflation-adjusted sales per employee and net income per employee, and indicated average increases of 11 and 32 percent respectively for the sixty-one enterprises after privatization. The study also indicated that investment, as measured by the ratio of capital expenditures to sales, increased 44 percent on average, after privatization. Output, measured by increases in real sales, increased 27 percent, on average, after privatization. The study's most surprising conclusion was that employment in the sixty-one enterprises actually increased, on average, by 2,346 employees, or 6 percent, following privatization. The study also showed that debt–equity ratios improved after privatization, and dividends as a percent of sales increased.

The efficiency and welfare gains from privatization, though, need a closer look in those cases involving the privatization of integrated monopolies—in many countries, the telecommunications and power sectors. Since privatization of integrated monopolies alone will not automatically increase competition in these sectors, governments must consider "unbundling" parts of the monopoly SOE; that is, identifying the segments of the monopoly that are potentially competitive (such as power generation for a power company) and promoting new entry and competition by the private sector in these segments. Yet an integrated monopoly will generally be more attractive to investors than an unbundled monopoly. The government, in its desire to gain privatization proceeds, may therefore decide against unbundling and sell off the monopoly at a premium. However, over time the loss in efficiency to the economy will outweigh any short-term gain from greater revenue.

The long-term efficiency gains from unbundling must still be weighed against the additional time which the unbundling process takes. The opponents of privatization may even call for unbundling a monopoly, using the unbundling argument to postpone privatization and extend state control. In this case, the benefits of even an imperfect privatization of an integrated monopoly would be better than continued state ownership. A guiding principle should be to unbundle as much as possible, but not to let it serve as an excuse not to privatize or to slow things down. For those sectors that cannot be immediately unbundled, time limits must be set on monopoly rights. This can encourage needed investment in the short term, and lead the way to more competition in the medium term.

Generation of Revenue to Reduce Deficits and Debt

Government budgets worldwide are stretched to the limit. Most governments around the world can only meet bills by raising taxes or by inflating the currency to reduce the real value of debt. However, taxes are already too high in most countries, and any increases will force more people and firms into the informal economy. Inflation damages financial markets and has other deleterious effects. Selling SOEs, on the other hand, is a viable way to augment government budgets. Privatizations generate revenue from the sale of shares in SOEs, eliminate the need to provide subsidies, and increase tax revenues from restructured and more productive enterprises. All these factors help restore fiscal balance and relieve inflationary pressures.

Privatization can ease a country's foreign debt burden, too. SOEs have been some of the main beneficiaries of government intervention, especially in terms of foreign debt. The World Bank's 1989 *World Development Report* notes that by 1986, "the outstanding stock of foreign loans to SOEs for a sample of 99 developing countries was twice that to the private sector. Borrowing was necessary not just for investment but also to cover losses."[24]

Lower deficits, achieved with the help of privatization revenue, reduces the government's need to borrow, which eases the "crowding out" of the private sector from financial markets. With privatization proceeds, reduced government demand for savings tends to reduce interest rates. Lower interest rates help all private sector firms, and can lead to an increase in share price for those firms that are listed.

Before privatization, some SOEs required huge subsidies which led to printing-press financing and inflation. After privatization, these SOEs face hard budget constraints and limits on credit from the banking system. This is crucial for reducing inflation and the uncertainty of financial transactions. Mass privatization may not raise revenue per se, but it can reduce the level of required subsidies. Once restructured, many enterprises become profitable and can contribute tax revenues to the budget.

Capital Market Development

One of the most important benefits of privatization is its impact on capital markets. It is useful to summarize some of the main points of this impact, which anticipate our discussion of capital markets in Chapters 3 and 4, where it is argued that capital markets can facilitate and contribute to saving, investment, and economic growth.

Privatization has a macroeconomic impact on the development of capital markets. As described in the preceding section, privatization of SOEs and economic infrastructure reduces deficits and inflationary pressure, which builds a stronger foundation for capital markets.

Privatization can be a means of deepening domestic capital markets. Public sale of shares, mass privatization, and BOO/BOT privatization lead to the creation of tradable securities. Public share sales and mass privatization help create broad and diversified share ownership, new companies listed on the stock exchange, and new investment funds. These forms of privatization stimulate the creation and scope of operation of capital market agents, including critical "back office" operations.

The usual candidate companies for privatization are just the ones needed to add liquidity and stability to the stock market. Many of the SOEs were created to give government control of the "commanding heights" of the economy. Although such SOEs invariably require restructuring after privatization, selling SOEs in the telecommunications, power, banking, petroleum, cement, and other sectors will increase market capitalization and liquidity, and add stability to the stock market.

Privatizations by share sale can help to transfer the financial technology of initial public offerings (IPOs) to the fledgling local securities industry, and have a demonstration effect by encouraging private sector companies to undertake their own IPOs and secondary offers to raise equity financing. These are new vehicles to channel savings into productive investment, which is a key to economic growth.

Privatization can also be decisive in developing local institutional investors, such as mutual funds, insurance companies and pension funds, which are critical to expanding capital markets and making them professional.

Attracting Foreign Investment

Developing countries are finding it increasingly important to attract foreign capital to achieve higher rates of
growth. Without foreign capital, the investment that fuels
growth will be limited to domestic saving. It is unlikely that
the financing role of foreign bank loans to those countries
that need it most will return to the levels of the 1970s. Official public assistance, especially at a time of fiscal con-
servatism by OECD countries, cannot be expected to fill
the gap. The additional foreign capital therefore must
come through foreign direct and portfolio investment.

Many countries that are privatizing would like to attract a strategic foreign investor into a SOE because such
investors can bring capital, new technology, new export
market access, and professional management to the
enterprise. A controlling block sold to a foreign investor
can be combined with a public share sale and shares allocated to management and workers on a preferential
basis. Attracting this kind of foreign investment is an important feature of many privatization programs, including those in Sri Lanka, Argentina, Chile, and Jamaica.
Privatization by BOT techniques, in particular, attracts
foreign direct investment. The huge levels of investment
needed in economic infrastructure have encouraged
governments to permit foreign and local private sector
investors to bid on infrastructure projects that otherwise
might not be built owing to budgetary limitations.

Privatization also encourages foreign portfolio investment. Portfolio investors in developed countries are attracted by the high returns in emerging markets and low
correlations with developed markets (which lowers their
overall portfolio risk.) A plethora of investment funds has
developed to give Western investors the opportunity to
access the capital markets in developing countries.
These funds include general emerging market funds,
regional funds, specific country funds, telecommunications funds, and infrastructure funds. Some funds spe-
cialize in purchasing the shares of companies being

privatized. Managers of these funds have directed billions of dollars to emerging markets.

Foreign portfolio investment in emerging markets increases demand for equities. This demand, other things being equal, will lead to stronger share prices, which will lower the cost of capital to companies wishing to issue new shares. In this way, foreign portfolio investment encourages new issues and new listings in developing countries. Foreign portfolio investors are an additional source of demand for SOE shares offered for privatization, although some governments may limit participation in privatization to local residents in order to avoid criticism that SOEs are being sold off to foreigners.

Foreign portfolio investors make the markets more efficient by using analytical techniques to buy undervalued shares and sell overvalued ones. They usually demand better information than domestic investors do, which may improve local investment research abilities, accounting standards, audit procedures, and disclosure requirements. Foreign portfolio investors have been instrumental in the emergence of emerging markets over the last decade (illustrated in Chapter 3 in Table 3.1): In 1985, net portfolio equity flows were $150 million to developing countries; in 1993, they were $46.9 billion, which was nearly as much as official development finance of $53.9 billion.[25]

NOTES

1. There are, of course, many risks and potential pitfalls that come with privatization. The type and techniques of privatization may not be correctly chosen, resources and political will and commitment may be wanting, and implementation may be weak. A full discussion of these issues is beyond the scope of this book; the discussion that follows assumes that these potential problems can be overcome. From a medium- to long-term perspective, the greatest political risk may be to do little or nothing to privatize and develop capital markets, and thereby promote growth, at a time when the economic aspirations of most people are growing.

2. World Bank, *The East Asian Miracle* (New York: Oxford University Press, 1993), 10.

3. This profile of problems with SOEs draws in part on World Bank, *World Development Report 1994* (New York: Oxford University Press, 1994), 37–40, and World Bank, "Infrastructure Regulation: Issues and Options," a paper prepared by the Private Sector Development Department, World Bank, Washington, D.C., October 1994.

4. E. S. Savas, *Privatization: The Key to Better Government* (Chatham, N. J.: Chatham House Publishers, 1987), 3.

5. World Bank, *World Development Report 1994*, 57.

6. The Cato Institute, *The Cato Handbook for Congress* (Washington, D.C.: The Cato Institute, 1995), 90.

7. For further discussion, see Savas, *Privatization*; Reason Foundation, *Privatization 1995* (Los Angeles,Calif: The Reason Foundation, 1995); Privatisation International, *Privatisation Yearbook 1995* (London: Privatisation International, 1995); and John D. Donahue, *The Privatization Decision: Public Ends, Private Means* (New York: Basic Books, 1989).

8. This discussion on Europe draws on Organization for Economic Co-operation and Development (OECD), *Financial Market Trends* (Paris: OECD, 1995), 13–30.

9 . OECD, *Financial Market Trends,* 21–23.

10. World Bank, *Bureaucrats in Business* (Summary) (New York: Oxford University Press, 1995), 1.

11. Paul Holden and Sarath Rajapatirana, *Unleashing the Private Sector: A Latin American Story* (Washington, D.C.: The World Bank, 1995), 76.

12. World Bank, *Argentina's Privatization Program: Experience, Issues, and Lessons* (Washington, D.C.: The World Bank, 1993), 2.

13. World Bank, *Bureaucrats in Business*, 6.

14. World Bank, *The East Asian Miracle,* 1–26.

15. Ibid., 354. This conclusion is based on the narrow definition of industrial policy as an "attempt to achieve more rapid productivity growth by altering industrial structure."

16. World Bank, *Bureaucrats in Business,* 6.

17. Ibid., 7–20, and World Bank, *Adjustment in Africa* (New York: Oxford University Press, 1994), 8–16.

18. World Bank, *Adjustment in Africa,* 1–8.

19. World Bank, *Bureaucrats in Business,* 6.

20. Ibid.

21 Ibid.

22. Ahmed Galal and Mary Shirley, eds., *Does Privatization Deliver?* (Washington, D.C.: The World Bank, 1994), 4–6.

23. William L. Megginson, Robert C. Nash, and Matthias van Randenborgh, "The Privatization Dividend: A Worldwide Analysis of the Financial and Operating Performance of Newly Privatized Firms," *Public Policy for the Private Sector,* The World Bank Group, December 1995, 33–36.

24. World Bank, *World Development Report 1989* (New York: Oxford University Press, 1989), 57.

25. International Finance Corporation, *Emerging Stock Markets Factbook 1995* (Washington, D.C.: The International Finance Corporation, 1995), 6.

CHAPTER THREE

CAPITAL MARKETS

Constraints and Opportunities

The first part of this chapter defines financial terms and explains the role of financial and capital markets in the economy. The next part discusses three reasons why financial markets, and especially capital markets, fail to live up to their potential in developing countries: a development strategy of intervention, the dominance of the banks, and the failure to adequately privatize the economy. The chapter concludes with a discussion of the benefits of capital markets.

CAPITAL MARKETS: DEFINITIONS AND FUNCTION

It is useful first to distinguish between real assets and financial assets. Real assets, which include land, labor, and capital, are used to produce the goods and services created by an economy. Financial assets are claims to the income generated by real assets. They do not contribute directly to the productive capacity of society per se; rather, they determine how the returns generated by real assets are divided among investors.[1] Financial assets which are liquid and easily accessible, and which offer returns commensurate with risk, encourage financial saving.

Actors in Financial Markets

The main actors in financial markets are households, businesses, and government. Households seek to diversify risk through a portfolio with both real assets (such as houses and land) and financial assets (such as a bank savings account, stocks, and bonds). Claims against future income can be held directly by households or through financial intermediaries such as banks, mutual funds, or pension funds.

Businessmen try to raise money to finance their investment in productive enterprises when their own internal funds are not sufficient. They can do this through debt incurred by borrowing from financial institutions or issuing corporate bonds, or by taking in new equity owners in the firm. In developing countries, SOEs usually financed their investment by accessing debt through commercial banks, from development finance institutions, and from foreign borrowing.

Governments must borrow money to raise funds when tax revenues are not sufficient to cover their expenditures. They cannot sell equity shares. They may be able to induce or compel bank funding which, in effect, is the same as printing money. However, this course of action is limited by inflationary implications. They can borrow money from abroad or from domestic savers, but this too is limited. A non-inflationary way to raise revenue is through selling government bonds to the non-bank public.

Government bonds, however, can be a mixed blessing, since they create a means to expand government spending beyond what is economically healthy. A better approach is to raise funds, reduce spending needs, or both, by shifting government activities to the private sector through the different forms of privatization discussed in Chapter 2.

Financial Markets: How They Work

Financial markets consist of groups of institutions and individuals who work to create and trade financial assets. Financial markets serve to move surplus savings (usually from households) to those economic units that cannot finance all of their activities from their own saving (usually business and government).[2] Businesses still finance much of their investment directly out of their own saving. Financial markets therefore intermediate only part of a country's total investment. If financial markets do this efficiently, they reduce the costs of intermediation; that is, of transferring resources from savers to investors. This efficiency increases the return to savers, and reduces the cost to investors.

Careful project selection by private sector intermediaries, such as banks, institutional investors, and securities firms, increases the productivity of investment and generates a positive real rate of return, which enables a positive rate to be paid to savers. Productive investment increases economic growth.

The reverse is also true. Poor decisions result in unproductive investments and a waste of resources and, ultimately, slower economic growth. The practical objection to government involvement in financing SOEs and other projects is that political and bureaucratic decisions tend to be based on non-economic factors (e.g., social or political objectives) and so result in many bad decisions, leading to poor projects with wasted investment and little or no contribution to growth.

Financial markets facilitate investment and are directly related to economic growth. Positive real interest rates favor financial saving over other forms of saving and therefore promote financial deepening. Greater financial depth, more investment, and faster growth all come partly from higher financial saving. Unfortunately, many governments have "repressed" financial markets by setting low and often negative interest rates to reduce borrowing costs for SOEs and favored projects, although this ultimately has an invidious impact on financial saving.

a sign of liquidity. There is no "correct" number as far as market turnover goes. However, in a stable, liquid market, turnover falls somewhere between the volatility of some exchanges and the sluggishness of other exchanges. Experience indicates that the privatization of well-known, blue-chip SOEs plays an important role in increasing market turnover, since these shares are broadly held and attractive to investors.

A formal stock exchange per se is not necessary for a secondary equity market. More informal "over-the-counter" markets can serve the same purposes at lower levels of trading volume. An over-the-counter market is a network of dealers who trade among themselves and the public. Over-the-counter markets are not uncommon in developing countries in the absence of an organized stock exchange.[6] In a developed market, a computerized dealer market such as the NASDAQ in the United States can provide healthy competition with the organized exchanges.

Emerging Stock Markets

In spite of the biases against capital markets, the emergence of stock markets in developing countries over the last decade is remarkable. In the late 1980s, emerging markets provided a new and promising investment theme for foreign portfolio investors. With economic reform, the economies, and many companies listed on the stock exchange, showed attractive long-run prospects. However, because the capital markets are underdeveloped, the share prices of listed companies were often low and therefore an attractive buy. Investing in emerging markets creates an excellent opportunity for portfolio diversification and reducing portfolio risk, because the correlation of the emerging market's return (capital gains and dividends) is low compared to that of developed markets. Emerging markets have become a respectable asset class for foreign portfolio investors in the 1990s, as evidenced by the existence of numerous emerging market funds.

What is an emerging stock market? The great heterogeneity of countries, economies, financial systems, regulatory regimes, trading procedures, and other variables does not permit an exact definition. Moreover, the boundary between developed markets and emerging markets on the one hand, and emerging markets and "pre-emerging" markets on the other, is often ambiguous.

The International Finance Corporation, the private sector arm of the World Bank, has taken a lead in promoting and developing emerging stock markets through advisory work with governments, collecting and disseminating data on these markets, and creating funds through which institutional and individual investors can participate in emerging stock markets. The IFC considers that all the economies that the World Bank classifies as "developing" are emerging markets, for even if they do not have a stock exchange, they have the potential to emerge at some point given the right set of economic policies.

The IFC currently collects data on fifty-nine emerging stock markets which are large enough to merit statistical attention, up from the thirty-two countries that it reported on in 1991—a reflection of the rapid growth in stock market activity in developing countries. Of these, twenty-six countries are in the IFC's composite index. Table 3.1 illustrates the "emergence" of this leading group of emerging markets from 1985 through 1994.

Tables 3.1 and 3.2 point to the good and bad news about emerging markets. Stock markets have indeed emerged, as Table 3.1 indicates, over the last decade, although 80 percent of all market capitalization for emerging markets is dominated by eight countries. Table 3.2 indicates that the majority of developing countries do not have stock markets of any significant size, and therefore do not have highly developed capital markets. The next section discusses why these markets have been, and continue to be, underdeveloped.

WHY CAPITAL MARKETS ARE UNDERDEVELOPED

In its survey of financial systems and development in the 1989 *World Development Report,* the World Bank noted that, "Many countries developed a market for short-term debt,

Table 3.1
Leading Emerging Markets (IFC Index Markets)

Market	Market Capitalization (US$ millions)		Value Traded (US$ millions)		Listed Companies	
	1985	1994	1985	1994	1985	1994
Argentina	2,037	36,864	631	11,372	227	156
Brazil	42,768	189,281	21,484	109,498	541	544
Chile	2,012	68,195	57	5,263	228	279
China	—	43,521	—	97,526	—	291
Colombia	416	14,028	30	2,191	102	113
Greece	765	14,921	17	5,145	114	216
Hungary	—	1,604	—	270	—	40
India	14,364	127,515	4,959	27,290	4,344	7,000
Indonesia	117	47,241	3	11,801	24	216
Jordan	2,454	4,594	163	626	104	95
Korea	7,381	191,778	4,162	286,056	342	699
Malaysia	16,229	199,276	2,335	126,458	222	478
Mexico	3,815	130,246	2,360	82,964	157	206
Nigeria	2,743	2,711	15	18	96	177
Pakistan	1,370	12,263	236	3,198	362	724
Peru	760	8,178	38	3,080	159	218
Philippines	669	55,519	111	13,949	138	189
Poland	—	3,057	—	5,134	—	44
Portugal	192	16,249	5	5,275	24	195
South Africa	55,439	225,718	2,836	15,954	462	640
Sri Lanka	365	2,884	3	700	171	215
Taiwan, China	10,432	247,325	4,899	711,346	127	313
Thailand	1,856	131,479	568	80,188	100	389
Turkey	—	21,605	—	21,692	—	176
Venezuela	1,128	4,111	31	936	108	90
Zimbabwe	360	1,828	9	176	55	64
Total	167,672	1,801,991	44,952	1,628,106	8,207	13,767
Total Emerging Markets	171,263	1,928,972	45,156	1,639,893	8,916	17,115
Developed Markets	4,496,503	13,256,635	1,600,569	7,981,853	17,792	19,061
Emerging Mkts. As Percentage of Developed Mkts.	3.8%	**14.6%**	2.8%	**20.5%**	50.1%	**89.8%**

Source: Derived from International Finance Corporation, *Emerging Stock Markets Factbook 1995* (Washington, D.C.: The International Finance Corporation, 1995.)

Table 3.2
Capital Market Development: A Global Overview

		A.	B.	C.	D.
	World Bank Income Grouping	Number of countries ...	...of which population > 1 million	Number of countries with stock markets tracked by IFC	C/B
Emerging Markets	Low	59	53	14	26.4%
	Lower middle	68	49	24	49.0%
	Upper middle	44	24	21	87.5%
Developed Markets	High	38	24	25	104.2%
	World	209	150	84	56.0%

Source: Derived from World Bank, *World Development Report 1995* (New York: Oxford University Press, 1995) and International Finance Corporation, *Emerging Stock Markets Factbook 1995* (Washington, D.C.: The International Finance Corporation, 1995).

but only a few have more than a rudimentary system for long-term finance. In sum, the financial systems of all but a few developing countries remain small and undeveloped."[7]

Three basic reasons account for the underdevelopment of financial and capital markets in developing countries: a development strategy of intervention, the dominance of the banking system, and the failure to adequately privatize the economy.

Development Strategy: The Cost of Intervention

Failed development strategy has resulted in underdeveloped capital markets. After World War II (which was also the time of independence for many developing countries), most governments decided to intervene in their economy and financial system, with the help of the international development institutions, to speed up the process of development. By contrast, the United Kingdom and the United States left industrial development and infrastructure (e.g., canals, railways, and public utilities) to the private sector in the nineteenth century. The need to finance these projects stimulated the emergence of private capital markets, which facilitated investment and stimulated modern economic growth.

In this century, governments in developing countries thought they could speed up economic growth by creating SOEs and providing finance to them at low interest rates. However, as discussed in Chapter 2, the SOEs foundered. Inefficient and unproductive, many SOEs required huge subsidies, which often undermined fiscal and monetary stability. This state intervention through SOEs and other vehicles stymied the private sector in industry, commerce, infrastructure, and finance. As a result, economies performed well below their potential.

Financial markets in most developing countries in the 1950s and 1960s consisted largely of foreign commercial banks, which provided short-term finance. Markets and instruments to channel saving into long-term productive investment were limited. Legal and regulatory issues were largely ignored, in part because government ownership seemed to obviate the need for them. Little effort went into improving accounting, auditing, and disclosure regulations.[8] Government policies deterred foreign direct and portfolio investment. Several factors, related directly or indirectly to government intervention, proved inimical to financial and capital markets:

- Government-controlled banks and development finance institutions, which directed credit and capital to SOEs and "strategic" projects, often on the basis of political connection and patronage rather than financial soundness.

- Interest rate controls, which discouraged savers from holding domestic financial assets and discouraged financial institutions from lending long term.

- Overvalued exchange rates and exchange controls, which encouraged capital flight and isolated economies from world markets.

- Monetization of the fiscal deficits, which led to inflation and uncertainty about real interest rates and made medium- and long-term finance from banks and corporate bonds impractical.

- Generally poor economic performance, which lessened the prospects for satisfactory return on capital.
- Taxes on corporate profits, dividends, and capital gains, and other policies which discriminated against equity financing.

The effort to develop capital markets must stress reform of these deleterious policies. For without developed financial and equity markets to channel domestic saving into productive investment, economic growth will be hindered and cannot be sustained.

David Gill, a prominent advocate of emerging stock markets, notes that during the 1960s and 1970s, most government officials in developing countries were of the opinion that financial markets had no significant role in economic development.[9] The role of corporate finance in development was also ignored. Little attention was paid to the distinction between debt and equity in financing enterprises and projects. Stock markets were suspect as "gambling dens" which would drain away financial resources from the real economy. The easiest and most available means of financing, therefore, was debt through government channels.

While governments occasionally embrace a stock exchange as a symbol of modernity, their efforts must go beyond constructing a shiny new exchange building (which, in any event, must be left to the private sector) as a symbol of financial prestige. Effective reform must address those factors which inhibit the development of private sector capital markets, and especially equity markets. The process of economic reform and restructuring that began in the 1980s has had a significant impact on the economies and financial systems of a number of countries, but much more remains to be done.

Domination of the Banking System

The domination of the banking system, and the failure to privatize the economy adequately are linked to the interventionist development strategy. They merit a separate discussion in view of their particularly injurious impact on the development of capital markets.

Banks and DFIs have dominated financial markets in developing countries. If the amounts of finance available for SOEs were too small and the maturities of loans too short, or if finance was not available for small and start-up firms, the solution was to direct the commercial banks to extend credit to them and to create DFIs. These approaches overlooked equity finance, private sector nonbank financial institutions, the risks of high levels of debt, and the possibilities for, and benefits of, privatization.

Moreover, the DFIs, like the SOEs, became non-performing political captives. A recent study of the private sector in Latin America by the World Bank concludes that the existence of DFIs "hampered the development of the financial markets, because other lenders could not compete with the subsidized terms offered, and undermined the repayment ethic, as many of the loans were not repaid."[10]

Governments and central banks prefer bank domination: It is easier to control the supply of money and credit and to secure power, prestige, and perquisites. Stock and bond markets threaten this status quo. In functioning stock and corporate bond markets, funds flow directly between individuals (and institutions) to companies that require finance, outside government purview. Hanke and Walters note the following:

To reduce the ability of the private sector to compete for national savings, governments suppressed private bond and equity markets through taxes, duties and overburdensome regulations . . . once a government decides to control credit policies and financial intermediation, it cannot allow private bond and equity markets to develop. After all, if they did, enterprises would have direct access to the nation's pool of savings, and the government would lose a source of seigniorage and its control over the allocation of savings.[11]

Although banks dominate, they are underdeveloped: Loans are of short maturities and intermediation costs are high. They cannot finance long-term investments for industry, commerce, or infrastructure. As a result, economic growth suffers.

In state-owned banks, debt collection is often lax, undermining financial discipline. Governments direct banks to lend for political reasons—often to unsound enterprises and projects—placing the financial system at risk. Privatization of banks, and competition among banks, can help to make them more efficient and competitive.

Competition is also needed between banks and the stock and corporate bond markets. Competition stimulates creation of a variety of financial institutions and instruments for savers and investors, who differ in desired amount, length, interest rate, and mix of debt and equity. Competition increases efficiency of intermediation between households that save and businesses that invest, reducing costs and stimulating investment and growth.

Equity markets compete with banks to provide finance to companies, but they also complement banks. Companies or projects usually require a mixture of long-term debt and equity. Lenders look for equity in the balance sheet of a company, and so the banks themselves should favor an equity market. After all, an equity market will reduce the risk of longer-term lending by the banks. Gill observes that, "Financial systems, and there are still many of them, that favor the banking system at the expense of the equity market are often doing damage to banking as well as impeding efficient economic growth."[12]

In a study of thirty developed and developing economies for the period of 1980 to 1991, Kemirguc-Kunt and Maksimovic, noting that banks are fearful of stock market development because it will reduce their business, find evidence that "initial improvements in the functioning of a developing stock market produce a higher debt–equity ratio for firms, and thus more business for banks. These results also suggest that in countries with developing financial systems, stock markets and banks play different, yet complementary roles. Thus, policies undertaken to develop stock markets need not affect banking systems adversely."[13] They also note that "an important role of the stock market is to aggregate information and thereby induce lenders to extend credit to firms whose stock is traded."[14] In a study of data on forty-one countries from 1976 to 1993, Levine and Zervos find that "even after controlling for initial conditions and various economic and political factors, measures of banking development *and* stock market development are robustly correlated with current and future rates of economic growth, capital accumulation, and productivity improvement."[15]

Failure to Adequately Privatize the Economy

Although progress has been made in privatization, the role of SOEs in the economy has not been substantially diminished in most developing countries, as we have seen in Chapter 2. This fact alone is a significant hindrance to the development of financial markets, because governments usually cordon off the SOEs from nascent capital markets.

Governments close more than just the SOEs to the private sector. Economic infrastructure, which, in addition to power and telecommunications, includes highways, ports, airports, bridges, water, and municipal services, is a notable example. Governments usually maintain a monopoly in the provision of these services, in spite of their failure to do so in a timely, efficient, and productive way. This failure can be a severe bottleneck to economic growth.

Many financial institutions, such as social security funds, pension funds, and insurance companies, could play a dynamic role in capital market development as institutional investors. However, government ownership usually reduces them to passive purchasers of low-yielding government bonds, which serves as another means of financing budget deficits.

BENEFITS OF CAPITAL MARKETS

This section examines in more detail the benefits which capital markets provide for economic growth, the financial sector, enterprises, and individual and institutional investors.

Economic Growth

Bencivenga, Smith, and Starr, in reviewing several studies, argue that it is "beyond dispute that there is a close, if imperfect, relationship between the effectiveness of an economy's capital markets and its level (or rate of growth) of real development." This relationship is fostered, they note, through increased liquidity, increased sharing of information, and specialization by capital market agents.[16]

Equity provides a higher return to savers over time than most other financial assets. A higher return encourages financial saving (and the return of capital flight) and channels it into productive investment, which promotes growth.

A well-functioning stock market assists privatization. Studies discussed in Chapter 2 have demonstrated that privatization improves the efficiency and productivity of SOEs, which, in turn, promote growth.

More Competitive Financial System

Capital markets invigorate the financial system. Equity lends balance to economies that are skewed toward debt. As has been discussed, equity markets compete with banks, but they also complement them. Strong balance sheets, which equity markets make possible, permit more bank lending. Even competitive banks cannot provide all of the finance that companies require. Enterprises need equity markets for their long-term financing. Equity improves efficiency and lowers risk in the financial system. Financial development promotes economic growth.

A stock exchange provides an efficient, transparent way to value an enterprise. Equity markets measure the risks and returns of enterprises and industries. They promote improved accounting and auditing standards, which are needed to provide adequate disclosure to outside shareholders. This enables capital markets agents to establish a reference for valuing other companies and new issues.

Equity markets help to broaden the ownership base, which can be tapped for future financing needs. Hanke and Walters argue that, "Stable financial systems and free and open capital markets have played a major role in the development of many advanced or rapidly developing countries. Free capital markets do not guarantee rapid development; other ingredients are needed. Nevertheless, an ossified financial system will inhibit or even stop development. Therein lies the hope for reform."[17]

Benefits for Companies

Companies usually cannot finance all investment from internal savings, and heavy bank lending would leave companies with too much debt on their balance sheets. Subsidized government loans usually are available only to favored borrowers, and also erode the integrity of the financial system. But equity provides long-term finance for enterprises and compensates the investor for risks taken.

Equity finance has several advantages over debt finance. The original amount at which the company sells a share is not paid back by the company. Dividends may be suspended if there are temporary downturns in business. In contrast, repayments of loan principal and interest are scheduled; failure to meet these schedules can result in grave difficulties for the company. Thus, equity provides a cushion for cash flow when a company needs it. (However, in order to compensate investors for the added risks, equity is usually more expensive for a company than debt. Taxes on corporate profits, dividends, and capital gains further increase the cost of equity.)

A stock market also makes financing for small and startup firms possible by providing an "exit" for venture capital; that is, a means to sell the ownership claim for cash. The entrepreneurs and their venture capitalists are able to sell shares at attractive prices. Thus, they are rewarded for their initiative and risk taking, and are able to use their original capital and any gains for new ventures.

Benefits for Individual and Institutional Investors

A lack of good ways to save encourages capital flight. Bank accounts typically fail to pay attractive interest rates to savers. Land and real estate weather inflation well, but the market tends to be illiquid and beyond the reach of all but the affluent. Shares in companies are more attractive for savers. A stock market enables new shareholders to own shares in many companies and spread risk. A stock market broadens the ownership base of large firms, improving the distribution of income and promoting "shareholder democracy." This enables people to save for long-term goals, such as their children's education or their own retirement. Individuals do not have to manage their portfolios themselves. They can save through professionally managed mutual funds and pension funds, which have potentially high returns.

Institutional investors are attracted by the rates of return and liquidity offered by equities. Pension funds and insurance companies typically have long-term liabilities and can afford to hold equities, which, though often volatile in the short run, historically provide a higher rate of return than other types of assets. Equities provide a means for diversifying portfolio risk across a number of companies, industries, countries, and currencies. A stock exchange provides a convenient and inexpensive way of buying and selling shares depending on the needs of the institutional investor.

NOTES

1. They may contribute indirectly by providing a more attractive abode for savings, and thereby eliciting more saving and investment than would otherwise occur. Moreover, a firm's productive base includes its cash. See Samuel Skogstad, "Policy Reform and the Transition from Command to Market Economy: A Conceptual Overview," Policy Research Center, Georgia State University, 1995.

2. This section on financial markets draws on World Bank, *World Development Report 1989* (New York: Oxford University Press, 1989).

3. In a financial sense, equity simply means ownership. Examples of equity securities include common stock, preferred stock, and options and warrants. Debt securities include bonds and convertibles. Non-securities, on the equity side, include private placements and venture capital; on the debt side, they

include loans, mortgages, and other asset-backed loans. Bonds are tradable securities where the borrower issues (sells) an I.O.U. to the investor. The issuer typically makes semiannual payments of interest to the bondholder for the life of the bond, and then repays the original principal, or borrowed money, at the maturity of the bond.

4. Derivative securities, such as options and futures, exist in some of the more advanced emerging markets, but they require a level of sophistication and financial information not typically found in most emerging markets. Therefore, they are not, in general, discussed in this book.

5. Investment banks may also agree to try to sell the shares on a "best efforts" basis, where they try to place the shares with investors but are not required to buy any unplaced shares.

6. In the literature and common parlance, these financial terms are not always used consistently. In emerging market countries, capital market development is usually synonymous with the equity market development. Some writers distinguish between capital markets, by which they generally mean the stock and bond markets, and the commercial banking system. In fact, given the fact that the maturities of most non-subsidized commercial bank loans are less than one year in developing countries, the banks often do not serve a capital market role. With economic reform, competition, privatization, and the development of equity markets, commercial banks can extend the amount and maturity of their loans into the capital markets segment of financial markets (for one year or more).

The title of this book could substitute "securities markets" for "capital markets." What is essential to capital markets is the development of a market for securities—readily tradable instruments that can be purchased by large and small investors, and which are, or have the potential to be, liquid instruments. The term "capital markets" has come to enjoy a certain popularity in describing, primarily, the development of stock markets, especially in Eastern Europe and the former Soviet Union. For ease of exposition, this book occasionally uses the terms "capital market," "equity market," and "stock market" interchangeably.

7. World Bank, *World Development Report 1989*, 2.

8. Ibid. 54–55.

9. David Gill, "Two Decades of Change in Emerging Markets," in *The World's Emerging Stock Markets*, edited by Keith K. H. Park and Antoine van Agtmael (Chicago: Probus, 1992), 49.

10. Paul Holden and Sarath Rajapatirana, *Unleashing the Private Sector: A Latin American Story* (Washington, D.C.: The World Bank, 1995), 63.

11. Steve H. Hanke and Alan A. Walters, eds., *Capital Markets and Development* (San Francisco: Institute for Contemporary Studies, 1991), 28, 39.

12. David Gill, "Two Decades of Change in Emerging Markets," 54.

13. Asli Kemirguc-Kunt and Vojislav Maksimovic, "Stock Market Development and Firm Financing Choices," policy research working paper 1461, The World Bank, Washington, D.C., May 1995, 4–5.

14. Ibid. 24.

15. Ross Levine and Sara Zervos, "Policy, Stock Market Development and Long-Run Growth" (Paper presented at World Bank Conference, Washington, D.C., February 1995), 1.

16. Valerie R. Bencivenga, Bruce D. Smith, and Ross M. Starr, "Equity Markets, Transactions Costs and Capital Accumulation: An Illustration," policy research working paper 1458, The World Bank, Washington D.C., 1.

17. Hanke and Walters, *Capital Markets and Development,* 42.

PRIVATIZATION AND CAPITAL MARKET DEVELOPMENT

This chapter discusses the elements of establishing a stock market and a stock exchange, which require simultaneous work on several fronts, including the following:

- Public awareness about the benefits and opportunities of a stock market and owning shares in companies, and how privatization contributes to this.
- Development of capital markets infrastructure, such as computerized trading systems; clearance and settlement; share registries; and capital markets agents, such as brokers and dealers.
- Development of a basic regulatory structure to promote public confidence and protect investors, emphasizing self-regulation.
- Privatization to promote the supply of, and demand for, shares.

The development of corporate bond markets is also briefly discussed. A full discussion of the elements of stock market development is beyond the scope of the present book.[1] This chapter focuses instead on some of the main points of capital market development as they relate to privatization.

The development of capital markets must be first and foremost a private sector activity. The government's proper role, albeit limited, is nonetheless key. In particular, government must be aware of the links between privatization and capital market development, and structure its privatization program to take advantage of these links. In practice, coordinated efforts to privatize and develop capital markets are rare. This makes for weaker privatization and capital market programs.

PUBLIC AWARENESS

A public awareness campaign sponsored by the government (but implemented by the private sector) is critical for both capital market development and privatization, as most people will not understand the benefits and objectives of a stock market or privatization. Of the two, privatization will probably be more controversial, with its suggestion of loss of jobs by workers (although empirical evidence discussed in Chapter 2 points out that, on balance, privatization leads to job creation). It is usually better to first highlight the advantages of a capital market, since a stock market is often seen as a symbol of prestige and share ownership can benefit almost everyone. Once the benefits of a stock market are explained, the need for privatization becomes clearer.

Public awareness was a key component in a project to develop capital markets in Sri Lanka. (It was complemented by a separate privatization project.) The public awareness component of the project developed advertisements in Sri Lanka's three main languages in the local newspapers, which described how the stock market works and how one could invest in shares. Respondents to the advertisements were sent a booklet describing how the Colombo Stock Exchange (CSE) operates. Articles about the stock exchange appeared in the national newspapers, and radio and TV interviews were conducted about the stock market. Training seminars were given to high school teachers to enable them to teach college preparatory courses in capital markets. An accompanying textbook, *A Guide to Share Market Investing in Sri Lanka,* was prepared, to be formally introduced into the college preparatory tracks of secondary schools.

A privatization by sale of shares presents the opportunity to explain not only the benefits of privatization, but also to serve as a primer on the basics of capital markets. In Jamaica, for example, the prospectus for Telecommunications of Jamaica included basic questions, with short, clear answers, including the following:

What is a share?

What is the prospectus?

If I decide to sell my shares later on, how would I do that?

Who is a stockbroker?

How can I benefit from owning shares?

What is a dividend?

Thus far, mass privatization programs have been utilized in former command economies where most people had only sketchy knowledge of how a market economy works. Public awareness is critical for developing "demand" for mass privatization by the population, building its confidence in capital markets and explaining shareholder rights and corporate governance responsibilities that come with share ownership.

In mass privatization programs with vouchers, the private sector investment funds play a crucial role in public awareness by advertising privatization and share ownership. An advantage of using vouchers in privatization is that the different funds compete among themselves to persuade citizens to let them invest the vouchers. In the former Czech and Slovak Federal Republic, the mass privatization program was listless until the funds began to compete actively to attract citizens' vouchers.

During Russia's mass privatization program, Russian television was saturated with advertisements from investment funds in competition to attract and invest the vouchers of Russian citizens in mass privatization auctions.

The government should establish guidelines so that the privatization funds do not promise more than they can deliver (guaranteed returns, for example). A lack of such guidelines can create subsequent controversy and problems for the program.

DEVELOPMENT OF CAPITAL MARKET INFRASTRUCTURE

Mark Mobius, a veteran manager of emerging market funds, points out that "back-office" operations of a stock exchange, such as clearing and settlement procedures for trades, can be counted on to work smoothly in most transactions in developed markets. However, in emerging capital markets, the smooth functioning of these operations can seldom be taken for granted. As a result, they assume "front-office" importance.[2]

Emerging market countries have the chance to supersede the trading systems of established capital markets by installing state-of-the-art technology in computer power and software. A key policy point is that the trading system, like the stock exchange itself, must be owned and operated by the private sector, lest budgetary and other limitations retard its development. Since there is no need for the trading system or other elements of the capital market infrastructure to be a government function, it should be privately owned, financed, and managed.

Trading Systems

The introduction of computerized trading systems, as worldwide experience demonstrates, has resulted in significant improvements in trading operations. Mobius summarizes the desired goals of a trading system with the acronym FELT:

Fair Both small and large investors should have equal access to shares at comparable prices.

Efficient The trading system must be established in such a way that paperwork is kept to a minimum and operations are conducted in the most direct and simple way with the lowest cost.

Liquid A trading system should foster high availability of shares on both the buy and sell sides. This also implies low transaction costs, which enable market participants to be active in the market.

Transparent The true nature of supply and demand should be apparent to investors so that they are able to judge the parameters within which they must work when completing their trades. This transparency fosters liquidity, fairness, and efficiency.[3]

Mobius argues that the way to meet the FELT objectives is through two mutually dependent requirements: computerized trading with automatic computer matching of trades, and centralization of the share registry and clearing and settlement arrangements.[4]

Share Registry

The share registry—a consolidated list of all shareholders in a company—is critical for determining shareholder rights, including receipts of dividends and corporate reporting, the right to vote for company directors, and other corporate governance decisions at shareholder meetings.

The share registry provides a link between privatization and capital markets and triggers secondary market activity. As part of a voucher mass privatization program, citizens go to the bid collection sites and fill out subscription-for-shares forms. These forms are collected and shipped to data entry centers. A computer processes the auction results and determines how many shares each bidder finally receives depending on the formula chosen to deal with the supply of shares in enterprises and the demand for their shares as expressed at the auctions. An official auction protocol is generated. Since the auction application forms were designed to capture all of the information required for the share registry, the auction results, as contained in the auction protocol, can serve as input into the share registry formation.

The other important initial component of the share registry is the employee's preferential share allocations. As discussed in Chapter 2, worker ownership can be an important benefit of privatization, and most governments offer shares to employees in SOEs on a preferential basis before shares are offered to the public at large.

The forms containing information on each component of preferential share allocation must be designed, as with the public auction process, in conformity with the share registry maintenance software. Thus, information on the preferential share allocation can be easily merged with information on the auction results and transferred to the company or the independent registrar. The baton is thus passed from the mass privatization program to the capital markets and enterprise restructuring. Accurate and reliable procedures for the transparent generation of the share registry from the auction protocol and the ensuing maintenance of the share registry are critical, because, without them, shareholder rights are placed in jeopardy.

Who should keep the share registry? Countries can use modern, efficient trading systems, featuring an independent, paperless, computerized Central Depository System, with a central share registry and central clearing and settlement. If it is not possible to move immediately to this system, then different licensed, independent share registrars should be required for enterprises above a certain number of shareholders. The disadvantage of keeping the share registry at the enterprise level was clearly demonstrated in the case of Russia's capital markets development. Because the directors of enterprises in Russia had direct access to the share registry maintenance, there was the opportunity for abuse—such as the simple deletion of undesired shareholders from the share registry.

Clearing and Settlement

Effective clearing and settlement procedures are required for a stock exchange. Clearing confirms the contract entered into by two brokers who execute a trade. Settlement ensures that the brokers exchange the funds for securities at a specified time and place.

The worldwide crash of stock exchanges in October 1987 exposed the risks and inefficiencies associated with inadequate clearing and settlement procedures. Following the crash, the Group of Thirty issued a standard set of nine recommendations for clearing and settlement. No country has met all of these recommendations. The United States, for example, meets six of the nine recommendations. But the Group of Thirty notes that, in general, progress is being made: "Settlement periods are shortening; securities are being immobilized or dematerialized in central securities depositories to facilitate transfers by book entry; and there is a particularly welcome emphasis on improving delivery versus payment procedures."[5]

The Group of Thirty has recommended that countries that are establishing share-trading, settlement, and clearing processes do so with paperless, book-entry dematerialized (i.e., dispensing with a physical certificate of ownership) shares. The advantages of this system have been alluded to: It is a faster, more efficient, and less costly procedure for share transfer.

Capital Markets Agents: Privatizing Privatization

An essential element of a developed capital market is a competitive industry of securities firms. A full discussion of this point goes well beyond the scope of this book, but it is important to note that privatizing the process of privatization can serve to stimulate capital market development by helping to establish capital market agents such as brokers and dealers, especially in "pre-emerging" and formerly planned economies.

The mass privatization program in Moldova, for example, consciously sought to utilize private sector firms in the various stages of implementation to help develop firms which would be well-placed to become capital markets agents, such as brokers and dealers, once mass privatization was over. Open, public tenders were conducted to select private sector firms to work as contractors to (the precursor agency to) the Ministry of Privatization and the technical assistance team. On this basis, six private sector firms were selected to assist in voucher distribution to Moldovan citizens.

The largest and most important tendering for private sector groups was for the operation of 115 bid collections sites throughout Moldova. The Ministry of Privatization undertook a national tender to select private sector firms. Their bid-collection experience will be invaluable in terms of setting up broker–dealer networks to trade shares after privatization.

Data entry centers are also operated by private sector groups selected by open tender. Additional private sector firms were competitively selected to work in small-scale enterprise preparation and the auditing of auction results. These contracts will stimulate capacity to perform audit functions, critical for capital markets activities. Capital markets require accurate financial information, and auditors play a critical role in providing an independent, third-party opinion on the reliability of data upon which so many key decisions regarding risk and return are made.

In the more advanced emerging markets, the participation of local securities firms in privatization is vital. Developed securities firms provide a set of related capital market services: They act as brokers and dealers, provide research and portfolio management services, and work with private companies to underwrite and sell new issues of their stocks and bonds and other securities to the public. The development of underwriting and placement services is key to developing a competitive securities industry. Participation in privatization by share sales help them develop this capability.

REGULATION OF CAPITAL MARKETS

Once they become aware of the benefits of share ownership, people need to feel confident that they will not be cheated if they participate in the capital markets.[6] Capital market agents demand transparency, honesty, and disclosure from companies, and they must, in turn, provide these to their customers. The need for establishing customer trust is especially keen when companies issue new shares (for example, following mass privatization) to raise capital for further restructuring and growth. When private companies offer to sell their shares, the public has to pay actual money for shares in enterprises for which the government has no responsibility, and will only do so if it has confidence in the integrity of the capital markets.

The regulation of capital markets involves creating self-regulatory entities that will establish an arbitration system and rules, membership rules, ethical standards of conduct, and related regulatory standards. These rules and standards will be drafted to provide fairness of process and investor and issuer protection and will enhance participants' ability to serve investors and issuers and compliance with securities law and related rules and regulations.

Some of the regulatory issues and areas that need to be addressed include investment funds and companies, registration of exchanges, broker–dealer registration, trading and sales practices, insider trading, corporate reporting, and registration of new issues. Other important issues include proxy solicitations, tender offer solicitations, and margin trading.

The framework for regulation is not static—it must evolve to deal with new problems and challenges. In the beginning, it must strike a difficult balance between providing safety to a public for whom dealing with capital markets is a new experience, while being careful not to overregulate a young market trying to get its sea legs. The regulatory framework must also be flexible enough to grow as the market matures and new problems arise. The wholesale importation of regulatory legislation from developed countries will not accomplish these objectives, and may actually hinder the development of the capital market through onerous requirements.

Nearly all capital markets have a mix of self-regulation by the stock exchanges and the securities industry, and government oversight. Given the limited administrative talent of government, and the skeptical, often cynical, view people have of government in most emerging market countries, it is advisable to stress self-regulation by private sector groups. Financial systems have languished for decades under government domination, and the investing public will be wary if government domination continues in the newly emerging capital markets. In a liberalized financial system, finance must be depoliticized as much as possible. Thus, regulation should be privatized to the fullest extent possible.

There are four basic elements to regulation of capital markets: individual self-regulation, industry self-regulation, competition, and independent government oversight.

Individual Self-Regulation

An effective way to discourage the behavior that regulation seeks to curb is to instill a sense of professional ethics in the individual capital markets agents. Developing an in-country program, such as the Chartered Financial Analysts (CFA) program administered by the Association for Investment Management and Research, would help to instill a sense of professionalism. This is a three-year program of self-directed study focusing on ethics, accounting, equity analysis, fixed-income analysis, portfolio management, economics, and statistics. The successful completion of three exams over a three-year period results in the award of the designation of Chartered Financial Analyst, a respected credential in the securities industry. In addition to promulgating individual self-regulation through professional ethics, the relatively low-cost course also transfers critical analytical skills needed to develop a professional capital markets industry.

Industry Self-Regulation

In some countries, responsibility for regulation of the securities markets rests primarily with the stock exchange. Members draft their own rules and regulations governing trading on the exchange, qualifications of members, and standards that members must meet.

The advantages of self-regulation over direct government regulation include greater ability to deal with problems owing to better remuneration and working conditions, and a clear interest in maintaining the confidence of the public in the capital markets. Self-regulation also tends to promote more rapid innovation in market practices and institutions. Off-the-shelf guidelines for stock exchange self-regulation in emerging markets exist and can be appropriately modified and utilized by emerging stock exchanges.

It is advisable to set up a group within the self-regulatory body for the capital markets to provide monitoring, compliance, and oversight of the critical capital markets agents. This should be an active unit which undertakes performance audits of investment funds, brokers, and dealers to detect and correct problems which could undermine confidence in a fledgling market. Of course, no system can completely eliminate scandals, and young capital markets must anticipate that these will occur. However, a monitoring and compliance unit can help to substantially reduce the number of problems.

Competition

Self-regulation can sometimes lead to anti-competitive behavior: for example, fixing prices on commissions and other services, restricting entry by new capital markets agents, and opposing changes which would improve efficiency in the industry, such as computerized trading. An important concomitant of self-regulation, both individual and industry, is competition to keep markets efficient and innovative.

In a free market, competition is the best regulator; a regulatory framework for capital markets must make use of competitive forces. Indeed, a reputation for probity and literally being an "honest broker" can be a source of competitive advantage.

Some markets have several stock exchanges, which promotes competition for listings among companies and participation by securities markets agents. In the United States, the computerized NASDAQ system is challenging the more traditional New York Stock Exchange and American Stock Exchange, and has largely eclipsed various regional exchanges. Deregulation of commission rates and a computerized FELT trading system will bolster such competition.

Foreign securities firms should be allowed to establish branches and subsidiaries in emerging markets. They are another source of competition in the capital markets and can help through training and work experience to transfer international standards more quickly to emerging markets.

Emerging market countries are increasingly recognizing that they are in competition with other emerging market countries for the available supply of direct and portfolio investment. Regulatory policies for capital markets and related areas must recognize that foreign investment will flow to those countries that have the fewest regulatory and tax barriers to entry and exit of capital.[7]

Government Regulation

Governments, having established the principles and regulations for investor protection and fair and efficient trading, tend to get involved directly in regulation to the extent that the capacity of the sources of regulation that have been described—individual self-regulation, industry self-regulation, and competition—is missing or inadequate.

It is important that the body charged with regulation and oversight be independent of any ministry or other executive or legislative office. The general principle of regulation in the United States is to create independent regulatory bodies, usually commissions, that become the cognizant government agencies. For example, in the United States, the Securities and Exchange Commission (SEC), the Federal Energy Regulatory Commission (FERC), and the Federal Communications Commission (FCC) are independent agencies headed by five voting commissioners who make independent decisions. The U.S. Congress created the SEC in 1934 as an independent, nonpartisan, quasi-judicial regulatory agency. The independence of these bodies makes it likely (though not certain) that regulations reflect economic rationality rather than political expediency.

Regulations which prevent or hinder foreign direct and portfolio investment, and make it difficult to obtain foreign exchange and repatriate it, impede capital market growth. As we shall see in Chapter 5, sometimes the best thing governments can do to develop capital markets is to change existing policies and regulations that impede their development. The "take-off" of the stock markets in Sri Lanka, Turkey, and other countries followed deregulation of this kind. It is also important to deregulate brokerage commissions and eliminate stamp taxes. Tax policy that discriminates against equity financing must be corrected. Analyzing data from forty-one countries, Levine and Zervos find that "stock markets tend to become larger, more liquid, more integrated internationally, and more volatile following liberalization of restrictions of capital and dividend flows."[8]

PRIVATIZATION: PROMOTING CAPITAL MARKETS BY INCREASING THE SUPPLY OF AND DEMAND FOR SHARES

In most developing countries, the shares of hundreds of SOEs are potentially available for the capital markets through privatization. Privatization of SOEs can play a leading role in supplying shares and creating a demand for shares by individuals and institutions.

In many emerging market countries which have a secondary market, trading is listless and the primary market moribund. Privatization of SOEs by share sale or mass privatization is often the first significant capital market transaction in many years. In a majority of developing countries and former command economies, neither a primary nor a secondary capital market exists previous to the privatization program. Thus, the privatization of shares (for cash or vouchers) in SOEs to the public is the first primary market activity in these countries.

Two types of privatization are well-suited to developing capital markets: broad-based share sales and mass privatization. The government can initiate broad-based share sales for a handful of "blue-chip" SOEs (i.e., the well-known, profitable ones that are attractive to the capital markets) to raise revenue and demonstrate professional IPO processes. Chapter 5 surveys the experience and issues with broad-based share sales.

Mass privatization can be used to divest the hundreds of mediocre and poor SOEs quickly, and to stem the government's loss through subsidies and the economy's losses through inefficiencies. Chapter 6 surveys the experience and issues with mass privatization. Mass privatization may also have a useful role to play in the privatization of economic infrastructure, such as telecommunications and power, as discussed in Chapter 7. In order to make privatization of these sectors not only palatable but also popular, the government can reserve a certain percent of shares (say, 5 to 10 percent) for the mass privatization program.

What is the mechanism by which privatization—either broad-based share sales or mass privatization—actually stimulates capital markets? Privatization allows the government to divest itself of shares and redistribute them to the private sector, that is, it creates shareholders. The private sector finds itself in possession of shares to be traded on the secondary market. Privatizing SOEs is thus critical to establishing this liquid and dependable secondary market so that shareholders have a means to buy and sell shares as needs and opportunities arise. Once secondary markets are established, the infrastructure is in place, and minimum regulatory framework has been set up, it will be possible for primary market activities to begin for the newly privatized firms and for private sector companies to raise new equity finance.

But even with a liquid secondary market, the number of private companies willing to offer and sell shares to the public on the primary market is a constraint to stock market development. Companies are often unwilling to "go public" through IPOs of shares and to list their shares on the stock exchange. They may be reluctant to widen the ownership of family owned and managed companies for fear of loss of control. This reluctance has limited new company listings.

Here again, privatization can have a salutary effect. A second mechanism by which privatization can stimulate capital markets is through the demonstration effect: Professional IPO processes as part of a government privatization program will show the way for private sector firms to sell shares to the public and list shares on the stock exchange, thus stimulating the primary markets. Similarly, the marketing effort that accompanies a well-run privatization share sale can be instructive to an emerging private sector financial community, which may learn from the marketing component of the privatization program that "deals are sold, not bought." In time, the reluctance of private sector firms to go public begins to ease as share prices on the stock exchange begin to find their proper level. If shares in enterprises are thus priced more efficiently, companies may find that equity finance is relatively more attractive than debt finance.

Governments need to take additional steps to privatize and deregulate the provision of economic infrastructure and to privatize institutional investors such as insurance companies and pension funds and social security to permit their full development as capital market agents. These points are discussed in greater detail in Chapter 7.

EMERGING BOND MARKETS

The development of a corporate bond market is an important facet of capital market development, one that typically comes after a stock market has been established.[9] The development of a corporate bond market indicates that lenders have confidence in assuming both interest rate risk over a long time and specific company risk. An active bond market reflects sophistication and stability in the economy and financial markets.

Stocks usually weather inflation better than other financial assets do, since most companies can usually pass on increases in the cost of inputs to customers by increasing prices, and thus maintain the real value of their cash flow and dividends. This makes it more probable that equities will develop first, and then corporate bonds after macroeconomic stability is achieved. Once enterprises have gone public with equity offerings, it will be easier to raise capital by selling corporate bonds.

A corporate bond market complements equity markets and leads to more complete financial markets in these countries. A bond market provides competition with the banks and equity markets. Bond markets enable companies to reduce financing costs relative to instruments such as bank loans and equities. Bond markets can facilitate the financing of massive investment needs of developing countries, especially for economic infrastructure which will be required to sustain high levels of economic growth (see Chapter 7). Corporate bonds are also attractive to institutional investors because of their predictable income stream.

Since corporate bonds are self-liquidating over time (unlike equities), the need for a secondary market in bonds is less compelling than for stocks. However, in order to develop capital markets, it will be desirable for the maturity of corporate bonds to lengthen. The longer the maturity of the bond, the more desirable is a liquid secondary market to sell these bonds well before the maturity date. Liquidity makes bonds more attractive to hold, and other things being equal, will lower the interest rate that enterprises will have to pay when they first sell them to the public.

NOTES

1. For a discussion of the elements of equity market development, see Brian L. Sudweeks, *Equity Market Development in Developing Countries* (New York: Praeger, 1989).

2. Mark Mobius, *The Investors' Guide to Emerging Markets* (New York: Irwin Professional Publishing, 1995), 111.

3. Ibid. 106.

4. Ibid.

5. Group of Thirty, "Clearance and Settlement Systems: Status Reports," a report prepared by Group of Thirty, Washington D.C. and London, 1992, 1.

6. For a fuller discussion of regulation of emerging capital markets, see Terry Chuppe and Michael Atkin, "Regulation of Securities Markets: Some Recent Trends and their Implications for Emerging Markets," The World Bank, WPS 829, January 1992.

7. The IFC's annual *Emerging Stock Market Factbook* contains information on withholding taxes for emerging markets, an investment regulations summary for entering and exiting emerging markets, an investment risk summary for entering and exiting emerging markets, and an information disclosure summary for emerging markets.

8. Ross Levine and Sara Zervos, "Policy, Stock Market Development and Long-Run Growth" (Paper presented at the World Bank Conference, Washington, D.C., February 1995),1.

9. For a discussion of emerging bond markets, see World Bank, *The Emerging Asian Bond Market* (Washington, D.C.: The World Bank, 1995).

CHAPTER FIVE

PRIVATIZATION BY SHARE SALE AND CAPITAL MARKETS

Western Europe, Latin America, and Asia

This chapter discusses the method of privatization which uses broad-based share sales to encourage "popular capitalism." This method, pioneered in the 1980s by the United Kingdom, has been implemented and modified in other Western European countries and in the emerging markets of Latin America and Asia. The method of broad-based share sales, besides securing the general benefits of privatization, has particular advantages for capital market development in emerging markets, even those with no or rudimentary stock markets. It creates a new class of investors, educates broad segments of the population about the advantages of a stock market, and can encourage the development of a fledgling securities industry. Finally, privatization by broad-based share sales is transparent, which reduces opportunities for cronyism and corruption.

PRIVATIZATION BY
BROAD-BASED SHARE SALES

A public, broad-based sale of shares is used to privatize a limited number of "blue-chip" SOEs (i.e., those that are the most attractive to investors). Not all privatizations by public share sales are necessarily broad-based. A public share sale is broad-based when the government uses techniques such as public awareness and favorable share prices to encourage the largest possible number of people to buy shares and become shareholders.

Many developing countries already have, or are eager to replicate, the broad-based approach to privatization. It has been adopted with varying degrees of success in several countries that will be discussed—Argentina, Chile, Jamaica, Korea, Malaysia, and Sri Lanka—as well as in Turkey, Tunisia, Portugal, and Venezuela. Other countries, such as Mexico and Thailand (also discussed), have instituted privatization programs which, as yet, have failed to take full advantage of the broad-based method.

To be sure, a broad-based share sale must be used with discrimination. The decision to broad-base depends on the quality and size of the SOE. Broad-based share sales require more time and money than a trade sale (or a share sale directed exclusively to institutional investors, which is usually not possible in emerging markets). Attracting a large numbers of applicants can be costly. Except for a certain number of blue-chip SOEs, a broad-based share sale will not be a good use of time or money. (SOEs in mediocre and poor condition are more likely candidates for mass privatization, while small-scale enterprises are best left to an open auction for cash sale.)

Even for attractive SOEs whose privatization by broad-based share sale would prove salutary for capital markets, governments may be under pressure to "get the deal done" quickly and easily by selling to a small number of traditional local investors (and perhaps a large foreign investor), rather than employing the broad-based approach. Still, governments must look beyond the short-term gain of a particular transaction and take advantage of the capital market implications of a privatization transaction.

Broad-Based Privatization and Capital Market Development

Broad-based privatization generates revenue for the government to reduce foreign and domestic debt, which eases fiscal burdens and reduces interest rates and pressure on the balance of payments. Annual tax proceeds to government after privatization are typically greater than any income generated by the firm as an SOE. As with some other forms of privatization, broad-based share sales can mobilize previously untapped savings and recapture flight capital. But the broad-based method can have particular advantages for capital market development.

Attractive Share Pricing As the owner of SOEs, governments can structure the privatization to meet broader objectives of capital market development. For example, a government can decide, in any specific privatization transaction, to accept less revenue (or incur greater expense and take additional measures) in order to create and develop capital markets. They might also do so as a way of bringing benefits of privatization to more of the country's population.

In a broad-based share sale, in which the government is using privatization to develop the capital markets, it is advisable to structure the share sale so that the price per share is attractive relative to value. An attractive price helps to achieve an oversubscription (i.e., more shares are demanded in the SOE than are available), which ensures the appearance of success and creates a healthy aftermarket for share trading. Success and strong secondary market trading are important to future share sales in the privatization program.

Attractive pricing of shares requires that the government be willing to forego some revenue. However, in a well-structured program, the revenue lost through underpricing in the first share sales can often be recovered, even exceeded, through higher prices in subsequent sales once the program is successfully launched (often because the capital markets develop quickly, equity is more attractive, and new share sales can be priced more highly). Success in each sale is vital to success in the next offering.

Increasing the Number of Shareholders Government policy that tries to spread broadly the benefits of economic adjustment and reform is sound. A feature of most privatization programs is an effort to spread share ownership, which builds support for the reform program. Broad-based privatization can create a new class of individual investors who will be able to support additional share offers of SOEs as well as public share sales of private sector companies.

In the mature capital markets of developed countries, the number of individual shareholders as a percent of the population typically ranges between 5 and 25 percent. By contrast, the number of shareholders as a percent of the population is minuscule in most emerging market countries. Before the implementation of privatization programs, there were only about 50,000 individual shareholders (0.2 percent of the population) in Argentina, 400,000 (less than 1 percent) in Thailand, 25,000 (less than 0.2 percent) in Sri Lanka, and 3,000 (about 0.1 percent of the population) in Jamaica.

As a result of privatization, Jamaica was able to attract 30,000 new shareholders in its first privatization alone, a tenfold increase, and Sri Lanka attracted an additional 25,000 shareholders, thereby doubling its base. Chile and Nigeria were able to attract 63,000 and 400,000 shareholders, respectively, as a result of privatization share sales.[1] The number of direct shareholders in Chile has since grown to several hundred thousand. Moreover, about 80 percent of Chilean workers have participated in the country's privatization of social security. These private pension funds have increasingly invested in equities since social security was privatized in 1981. Consequently, several million Chileans have become shareholders in this way. (These results, impressive as they are, pale in comparison with the results of mass privatization, which in Czechoslovakia and Russia created 8.5 million and 40 million new shareholders, respectively, where virtually none had existed before.)

Developing Investment Banking and Underwriting The expansion of a country's base of shareholders also benefits the local securities industry. The trading of the shares from privatization will be of obvious importance to brokers and dealers. However, the number of trades and the commissions from trading have limited revenue potential. To develop, these firms will need to find new sources of revenue. One possibility exists in the investment banking opportunities presented by privatizations of SOEs and new equity issues of private companies.

In emerging market countries, private companies that would like to sell shares to the public are constrained by the underdeveloped state of finance and underwriting activities. Because so many companies are financed either by directed credit, or limited to retained earnings and short-term working capital, the local expertise to take private companies to market has not had opportunity to develop.

In 1991, as Argentina stood on the cusp of its remarkable accomplishments in economic liberalization and privatization, the interest from private companies in raising equity was quite limited. This was attributed, in addition to the reluctance of Argentine owners to go public, to a lack of knowledge on the part of local financial institutions on how to structure a share sale. Professionally managed privatizations by broad-based share sales are a means of overcoming these constraints and developing investment banking. The growth in underwriting business which can accompany a privatization program also boosts the volume and quality of business for the securities industry. Several developing countries have been able to secure underwriting for their privatizations by share sales. Indeed, it is advisable to have the share sales underwritten because the application list may have to be held open for a relatively long period to accommodate unsophisticated, first-time investors. During this period, a number of problems can arise.

In some countries, potential underwriters may charge prohibitive rates. This was the case in the first two privatizations by share sale in Jamaica, precluding the use of underwriters. By the time of the third privatization, Telecommunications of Jamaica (TOJ), however, it was possible to secure underwriting at a reasonable commission because of the experience gained by financial institutions in observing the first two privatizations. TOJ was also a solid business prospect. (Underwriting turned out to be a prescient choice for the government, since the devastating Hurricane Gilbert struck while the application list was open. However, at the end of the application period, the shares were still oversubscribed.)

As a part of the broad-based effort, the privatization team must often create new networks to sell shares. Later, these can be utilized by securities firms for future privatizations and IPOs of privately held companies. Once privatization programs spur securities firms to begin to develop their professional capacity, the industry will be on its way to a more diversified revenue base. As these firms' sophistication grows, they will enhance their role in channeling saving into productive investment.

As investment banking and underwriting skills develop, governments—and private companies—will have to worry less about under- and overpricings. The development of bookbuilding capabilities, where the underwriters attempt to gauge likely demand from institutional investors before setting a firm price, will reduce the risk of underwriting. However, as the case of France demonstrates, developing these skills takes time. Fortunately, perspicacious governments can use privatization to speed up the development of such skills.

Transparency Broad-based share sales are perhaps the most transparent form of privatization. The issue of transparency—or the appearance of transparency—often does not receive enough attention by those in charge of privatization programs, even though failure to pay attention to transparency can delay a privatization program. Trade sales have often been criticized because procedures and evaluations of proposals lacked clarity and transparency, leading to suspicions of favoritism, cronyism, and possibly corruption.

In the broad-based process, a prospectus is made available to the public which provides relevant information on the company's history, management, business strategy, and financial performance for the last two or three years. The instructions for bidding on shares are also provided, along with application forms. Additional inserts can promote public awareness and provide information on what share ownership means. Computers determine the outcome of the share sale and allocate shares according to predetermined algorithms. The results can be audited against stated procedures to monitor compliance.

The remainder of this chapter highlights lessons from the experiences of countries in Western Europe, Latin America, and Asia with public share sales, many of which used the broad-based method.

WESTERN EUROPE

The British and French experiences in the 1980s demonstrate that privatization can broaden and deepen capital markets. Other Western European countries, such as Italy, Spain, and Denmark, are employing these techniques to advantage in the 1990s.

The United Kingdom: Pioneering the Broad-Based Share Sale

Many of today's privatization programs find their origins in the United Kingdom.[2] During the 1980s, the United Kingdom demonstrated to a skeptical world how a program to privatize large SOEs through a broad-based share sale could be successfully carried out. The privatization program enlisted the United Kingdom's developed capital market to facilitate the sale of its large SOEs. In turn, privatization broadened and deepened the United Kingdom's capital markets. A parallel program to sell government-owned housing to tenants also proved popular, and reinforced the awareness of the benefits of privatization.

The use of broad-based privatizations by share sales began in earnest in the United Kingdom in 1981, with the sales of British Aerospace and Cable & Wireless. Others followed quickly. The landmark privatization of British Telecom (BT) in 1984 made international headlines and served as a model for other countries. The British government offered just over 3 billion shares of BT for sale, representing 50.2 percent of the issued share capital. Of the total share offer, 415 million shares were offered to foreign investors.

At the time, critics doubted that an offer of that size could succeed. Key features of the share offer were the broad marketing of the sale and attractive pricing of shares to encourage as many individuals as possible to participate. The shares were sold at a discount to the market price–earnings ratio. It was targeted, in addition to U.K. institutional and foreign investors, at U.K. citizens who had never owned shares before, including BT's employees, BT's large subscriber network, and the general public. The employee share participation plan, which featured free, matching, and priority shares, helped ensure the support of the employees. Gross proceeds from the sale were nearly 4 billion U.K. pounds. The share sale brought 2.5 million shareholders to the market, 1 million of whom had never owned shares before.

British Telecom and the other U.K. privatizations, such as British Gas and British Airways, demonstrated a very positive side benefit in the increase in the breadth of the pool of shareholders, effectively creating a new class of investors. It is estimated that well over 7 million individuals became shareholders as a result of the privatization program. The government's success in spreading share ownership among private investors makes it unlikely that any future government would want or be able to renationalize these enterprises.

Financial deregulation and privatization has helped London to re-emerge as one of the world's top three financial centers, along with New York and Tokyo, despite the relative weakness of the U.K.'s economy vis-à-vis other Western European countries.

France: Using Privatization to Introduce New Offering Techniques

The French program, arising from a different set of circumstances, had goals similar to the British program and emulated some of its methods. After World War II, France began to nationalize some of its basic industries. In 1982, at a time when the rest of Europe was looking critically at its SOEs, President Mitterand and the newly elected socialist government decided to increase the number of SOEs. Despite initial enthusiasm, it quickly became apparent that this was a misguided policy.

From 1986 to 1988, President Mitterand was forced to share power, and a conservative coalition embarked upon a privatization program. Within a year and a half, it had "reprivatized" twenty-three enterprises, including Paribas and St. Gobain, for about $17 billion. The aims of the program were to promote "popular capitalism," to get employees more involved in their firms, and to make the French economy more competitive. The number of shareholders in France increased by about 5 million.[3]

In 1993, President Mitterand again had to share power with the return of more conservative politicians to the government. France resurrected its privatization program and modified the 1986 privatization law. Marquardt and Clarke illustrate how this modified law and program has "dynamized French capital markets" and has used privatization as a "legal laboratory" for testing share placement and distribution techniques.[4] A major goal was to use the revived privatization program to enhance Paris's standing as a financial center in Europe. The privatization law featured new offering techniques, common in the United States but not known in France, used by the offeror and underwriting syndicate to gauge demand by institutional and individual investors before setting the share price of the SOE being privatized. These techniques include bookbuilding and the pre-marketing mandate.

Bookbuilding is a technique for gauging institutional investor interest in a particular share sale by taking nonbinding orders or indications of interest from institutional investors, based on a preliminary prospectus that makes no reference to offering price. The investors respond with an indication of their interest at different possible prices. This knowledge of likely interest in buying shares reduces the risk for the investment bank in underwriting the share sale. Bookbuilding was used for the first time in France during the 1993 privatizations. In contrast to the previous French placement system, considered risky by American underwriters, bookbuilding opened the international capital markets to placement of shares in French privatized companies worldwide.

The pre-marketing mandate technique for individual investors was used for the first time in France during the privatization of the Banque Nationale de Paris. This technique enables individual investors to sign a purchase mandate to buy shares conditionally, without an agreed price in the company to be privatized. Once the offering price is announced, the individual has the right to revoke the mandate by a specified deadline, after which the mandate becomes irrevocable. Pre-marketing has proven to be a successful means of gauging private investor interest in the share to be offered.

Other Western European Countries

The privatization revolution of the 1980s in the United Kingdom and France is continuing in those countries and spreading, in the 1990s, to other European countries. Most European countries now plan large public sales of shares during the remainder of the century, which will raise large sums of money on Europe's capital markets and through international sales.[5]

Western European privatizations amounted to nearly $51 billion in 1994, and were expected to reach $40 billion in 1995. In 1994, the largest privatizations were undertaken in France ($10.7 billion), Italy ($9 billion), the United Kingdom ($8.5 billion), and Denmark ($5.7 billion). The OECD has estimated that proceeds from privatization in Western Europe could reach $200 billion over the next five years.[6]

Still, many of Europe's capital markets are underdeveloped, as indicated by such measures as market capitalization as a percentage of GDP. Greece and Portugal, in fact, are still considered to be emerging markets, based upon their per capita GDP. Many of these governments hope to use the privatization of their medium and large SOEs to develop their capital markets and improve their economies.

The need to sell large numbers of shares through privatization programs has induced Western European governments to modernize domestic securities markets and strengthen domestic institutional investors, especially insurance companies, by enabling them to buy equities rather than just government bonds and distribute increasing proportions of equity internationally, thereby promoting the globalization of capital markets.

These new offerings will increase market capitalization in Europe. In Italy, privatization by sale of shares could increase capitalization by 30 percent. In France, the privatization program has been estimated to amount to more than 10 percent of market capitalization at the end of 1994.[7] Large privatized enterprises should increase market liquidity, an attractive feature for institutional investors. Possibilities for diversification among companies and sectors will also increase significantly.

LATIN AMERICA

The experiences of some countries in Latin America and Asia in privatization and capital market development are similar to those in Western Europe. When privatization began in the late 1980s and 1990s, stock markets existed in many Latin American countries, although they were undeveloped and small relative to the economy. Privatizations, including broad-based share sales, have made use of these stock markets to divest large and well-known enterprises. Consequently, the market capitalizations of these stock exchanges have soared and, subsequently, made equity financing a more viable option for private companies.

Argentina: Privatization as Centerpiece of Reform

At the turn of the present century, Argentina was one of the world's most prosperous countries. But by mid-century,

President Juan Peron's interventionist policies, including the creation of SOEs, resulted in chronic deficits and inflation and sent the economy and capital markets into a slump for several decades. By 1989, Argentina was in the throes of a crisis caused by large deficits and foreign debt, hyperinflation, and a stagnant economy. Argentina's SOEs were inefficient and a drain on the budget: Financial results for the thirteen largest SOEs (excluding defense industries) showed an operating deficit of $3.8 billion on revenues of $8.7 billion in 1989. The World Bank, convinced that only radical change could address the inefficiencies, overstaffing, and general poor performance of SOEs, ceased lending to Argentine SOEs after 1988.[8]

President Carlos Menem, who came into office in July 1989, made privatization a centerpiece of economic reform. Privatization provided a source of funds to address the fiscal deficit and foreign debt problem. The government also wanted to make the SOEs more competitive and increase the efficiency of new investment in them.

After beginning its privatization program with several small transactions, the Menem government privatized the telephone company, ENTEL, Aerolineas Argentinas, and two television stations in 1991. By 1994, the federal government had privatized virtually all of its SOEs, including those responsible for electricity generation, transmission, and distribution; natural gas distribution and transportation, and its national petroleum company, YPF.[9] The privatization of YPF is the largest in Latin America to date and yielded $3 billion in proceeds. YPF, Telecom, and Telefonica are traded as ADRs in New York, making Argentina once again a part of international capital markets.[10] Privatization has reduced the federal debt by some $15 billion, and is also expected to save the federal budget at least $1.5 billion annually through the reduction of subsidies to SOEs.[11]

Privatization has contributed to capital market development by providing shares in the privatized companies. During the period of reform, from 1990 to 1993, Argentina's capital markets raised $9.9 billion in share sales, of which $5.3 billion consisted of privatization proceeds. Prior to this period, the Argentine securities markets had been moribund, generating only an annual $26 million of capital between 1981 and 1989. Argentina's stock market capitalization has grown from $2.0 billion in 1985, to $3.3 billion in 1990, and to $36.9 billion in 1994.[12] Stanley notes that privatization has stimulated new issues. Citibank floated a new issue of shares of a subsidiary holding company in Argentina that had acquired newly privatized assets.[13]

The Argentine government has also recently privatized its social security system along the lines of Chile's reform (to be discussed in detail in Chapter 7), to replace its current troubled system. The new pension system began operating in July 1994. Workers can choose between the state system or a private system. The private system can invest up to 35 percent of contributions in shares of companies listed on the stock exchange. The government expects this private social security system to develop Argentina's capital markets further.[14]

The government has also taken steps to liberalize the capital markets. In 1991, it eliminated the capital gains tax for foreigners, lifted limitations on holdings and time of investment, and provided for free entrance and exit through the foreign exchange market. Other measures include the deregulation of brokerage commissions, elimination of the stamp tax, and elimination of tax on cash dividends.

President Menem's reforms have reshaped the economy. Hyperinflation has been arrested and economic growth accelerated. Prices, products, and financial markets are substantially deregulated. Foreign investment and exchange controls have been liberalized.

Chile: Leader in Privatization of SOEs and Social Security

Chile's privatization experience is remarkable for its early start; for the large number of affected companies; and for its highly successful privatization of the social security system, an innovation generating ever-greater interest from developed and developing countries alike.

Chile began its privatization program in 1973 as part of a sweeping program of economic reform and restructuring. Toso identifies four stages in Chile's privatization program.[15] In the first (1974 to 1979), companies that had been nationalized were reprivatized, usually to former owners. The second stage witnessed a resumption of control of most of the country's important companies following an economic and banking crisis in the early 1980s.

In the third stage, financial reforms were undertaken to modernize the banking system and the capital markets. The government developed a mechanism called "popular capitalism" which, through a series of tax incentives, permitted a large number of small investors to participate in the privatization process through share purchase.

In the fourth stage, the government privatized companies that had been created by special laws and had been in the public sector for a long time, including the telephone company, the electric company, the steel company, and others.

Chile's privatization program actually preceded the United Kingdom's. However, because Chile's economic reforms were associated with the military government of General Pinochet, and its first privatizations suffered some reversals, the Chilean program did not serve as a model for other countries at the time. Under the new civilian government, privatization has continued, though at a slower pace. Polls indicate that privatization has won the acceptance of the majority of the population. Competition among privatized SOEs has improved, especially in the utilities sector.

Privatization has had a major impact on the growth and development of the Chilean stock exchange. Stanley cites data to show that "privatized companies do not just provide a bubble of transactions volume at the time of their privatization and initial trading on the exchange, but continue to be an active and important component of the market."[16]

One of Chile's lasting contributions to the art of economic reform is its bold and creative privatization of its social security system in 1981. This placed Chile in the vanguard of attempts to reform a serious problem facing, or soon to face, almost every country in the world. Many other countries have carefully studied Chile's innovative and successful privatization of its social security system, which is discussed in more detail in Chapter 7.

In 1994, Chile enacted a capital markets reform bill which cleared the way for pension funds to invest in equities traded abroad. The measure eased restrictions on pension fund investments, improved financial market regulation, and helped to develop new financial instruments through securitization.

Chile also plans to utilize public–private partnership techniques such as BOO/BOT privatization. The government plans to raise $200 to $300 million a year by selling concessions to private companies to build and operate economic infrastructure projects.[17]

Mexico: Successful but Narrowly Based Privatization

Mexico has used privatization successfully to address the economy's fiscal imbalance. However, the narrowly based program has failed to reap the benefits of a more broad-based share sale program.

Following its debt fiasco of 1982, Mexico adopted reforms to promote the private sector and outward-looking trade and industrial policies and reduce fiscal deficits and inflation. Key to these reforms was the privatization of SOEs. Through various means, the government reduced the number of SOEs from 1,155 in 1982 to about 200 in 1994. Many of the remaining SOEs are small or non-profit undertakings, although the public sector retains a few important SOEs, such as the national oil and railway monopolies and the national power company.[18]

The landmark privatization of Telefonos de Mexico (Telmex) occurred in a two-phase process. First, a controlling interest of Telmex was sold to the consortium of Grupo Carso (a Mexican diversified company), Southwestern

Bell, and France Telecom in December 1990. The government subsequently sold all but 10 percent of the company through an ADR in May 1991. At the time, this equity issue was the largest equity offering ever made by a developing country. Telecommunications service has improved as the controlling shareholders have set specific benchmarks for service quality and development of the network, including line growth of 12 percent a year. All towns with populations of 500 or more were required to have telephone service by the end of 1994.

Telmex's success encouraged the government to privatize eighteen government-held commercial banks during 1991 and 1992 for a total of $12 billion. These privatizations have been criticized for excluding foreign banks, which would make the sector more competitive, and for selling the banks to wealthy local groups. (However, NAFTA now encourages foreign participation in banking.)

Mexican privatizations did not have the participation of individual investors, or "popular capitalism," as a goal. Many of the privatizations were transacted in such a way as to perpetuate and even increase the concentration of wealth.[19]

The privatization program has had important positive implications for the government budget. From 1984 through 1992, the proceeds from privatization were about $20 billion. Privatization helped to retire public debt, and has enabled the government to reduce fiscal transfers to SOEs from 3.7 percent of GDP in 1983 to 0.8 percent in 1992.[20]

With a market capitalization of almost $130 billion at the end of 1994, Mexico's stock market is larger than those of many other developed countries. At the same time, the Mexican stock market still faces some typical emerging market growing pains: The market is relatively shallow and lacks liquidity.

Under the Salinas administration, Mexico projected the appearance of stability and sound economic management, and served as a model to other Latin American countries. President Salinas and his economic team received high marks as they reformed the economy and privatized the country's large portfolio of SOEs. However, political and economic problems emerged in 1994, after the government implemented unwise fiscal and monetary policies to stimulate the economy before an election. These led to a sharp devaluation of the peso which eroded the confidence of foreign markets. The sharp fall in the Mexican stock exchange, and a spillover fall in other emerging markets, were harsh reminders that the high returns enjoyed by local and foreign portfolio investors are attended by significant risk. After some time, the international markets realized that Mexico's short-term problems did not necessarily auger poorly for other emerging markets.

The underlying economic fundamentals in Mexico are strong thanks to privatization and other reforms carried out in the 1980s and early 1990s. However, failure to build a more broad-based public participation in the benefits of privatization has compounded the country's political problems and slowed the development of the country's capital markets.

The current Zedillo government has announced that privatization will focus on economic infrastructure, including railways, ports, electricity plants, satellite communications, and secondary petrochemical plants owned by the state oil monopoly, Petroleos Mexicanos (Pemex).[21]

Jamaica: The Broad-Based Model in a Rudimentary Capital Market

Jamaica, in the mid- to late 1980s, provided persuasive evidence that the U.K. broad-based privatization model can work well when transplanted to countries whose economies and capital markets are much less developed.[22]

In the mid-1980s, Jamaica's financial sector was relatively competitive and diversified. It consisted of the Bank of Jamaica, commercial banks, merchant banks, building societies, credit cooperatives, development banks, and insurance companies. However, Jamaica's securities market had lagged behind the rest of the financial sector.

Although Jamaica had a stock exchange, the primary market for securities (stocks or bonds) did not play an important role in financing the three basic types of companies in Jamaica. Financing of the subsidiaries of multinationals had generally occurred through international and domestic banks, loans from the parent company and retained earnings. Enterprises within the medium- to large-sized Jamaican holding companies relied upon domestic banks and the holding company. Smaller enterprises used family capital and internally generated funds.

The Jamaican Stock Exchange had been created in 1969. At first, the common shares of thirty-four companies were listed. This number increased to forty-one companies in 1973, but then fell to thirty-two during the period of Prime Minister Michael Manley's first administration, which placed a heavy emphasis on nationalization and government intervention. During the remainder of the 1970s, activity on the stock exchange was generally listless as the economy stagnated under the Manley socialist program, international oil shocks, and other adverse domestic developments.

In the mid-1980s, however, there was a significant rise in the stock exchange index, and volume and value of transactions. The strength of the stock market was based on economic recovery and the policy reforms of the Seaga administration, a related growth in corporate earnings, a perception that corporate equities were undervalued, and fairer tax treatment of equity as a part of Jamaica's comprehensive tax reforms. The increase in volume and value of transactions was also assisted by the privatizations by share offer, and subsequent listing on the stock exchange, of three large enterprises: the National Commercial Bank (1986), the Caribbean Cement Company (1987), and Telecommunications of Jamaica (1988).

In 1986, the Jamaican stock market only had about forty listed companies, with thin and erratic trading volume. As a result, it was open for trading only twice a week for two hours per session at the time of the share sale of the National Commercial Bank (NCB), the country's largest bank. There had been only two minor share offers in the preceding decade. At the time of the first privatization by broad-based share offer, the market capitalization of the Jamaican Stock Exchange was only about $500 million.

The NCB privatization was modeled along the lines of British Telecom, and sought to establish a broad base of shareholders. In December 1986, the Jamaican government sold 51 percent of NCB, the country's largest bank. This public offering was by far the largest in Jamaica's history. A key objective of the NCB privatization was broad-based share distribution to the Jamaican population. This was facilitated by attractive pricing, favoring individual buyers relative to institutions, and a beneficial employee share plan. The share sale was 170 percent oversubscribed and attracted more than 30,000 individual applications from Jamaican citizens and institutional investors, including 98 percent of the Bank's own employees. Prior to this, there had been about 3,000 share holders in Jamaica.

This was followed in successive years by the privatizations of the Caribbean Cement Company and Telecommunications of Jamaica. The offerings were politically popular and increased the market capitalization by approximately 20 percent. These share offers showed beyond a doubt that the U.K. broad-based model could work in a much smaller market, and dispelled the notion that underdeveloped capital markets, in themselves, are an impediment to privatization by share sale.

When Michael Manley returned to power in 1989, the socialist rhetoric and practices of his earlier tenure were of historical interest only. In the intervening period, he had become a leading proponent of privatization because it had proved to offer a solution to some of Jamaica's economic challenges. His party has continued the reform effort, including privatization. It has also abolished foreign exchange controls.

From 1988 to 1994, privatization of Jamaican companies resulted in seventeen trade sales and share sales, raising $253 million over the seven-year period. In 1992, the IFC identified Jamaica as the best performing emerging market in the world. Over the twelve-month period of 1992, the JSE share index increased in value by 235 percent.[23] In 1995, the government sold the national airline, Air Jamaica, and sold four of five state-owned sugar mills to local and foreign investors. The Jamaican government currently plans to sell the island's only oil refinery, Petrojam.[24]

ASIA

Korea: Liberalizing with Equity Finance and Broad-Based Privatization

Korea's privatization program, one ingredient in the country's overall drive toward liberalization, has helped promote equity finance for private firms, reducing their high debt–equity ratios.

The Korean stock market grew dramatically in the 1980s. In step with Korea's emergence as a newly industrialized country, the Korean stock market capitalization at the end of 1994 was $192 billion, making it one of the ten largest markets in the world.[25] Korea's stock market has played an increasingly important role in mobilizing savings. Created in 1956, a few years after the devastation of the Korean War, the Korean stock market became the principal source of capital for Korean corporations during the 1980s.

Korea, whose export-led growth strategy had enabled it to reach a per capita income of $7,660 by 1993, had tilted the financial field heavily in favor of debt as a part of its development strategy. The government allocated loans with subsidized interest rates to the *chaebol* (the large conglomerates) through the state-controlled banking system. However, years of preferential access to bank loans left *chaebol* companies with high debt–equity ratios. The average debt-equity ratio of firms in the industrial sector in Korea increased from about 1 in the early 1960s to about 5 by the 1980s.

The government, realizing that financial reform was a necessary ingredient for maintaining long-term growth, undertook measures to provide for increasingly market-determined interest rates, greater banking autonomy, privatization of its commercial banks, and the development of stronger equity markets. The Ministry of Finance encouraged the *chaebol* to raise capital in the stock market to reduce their debt–equity ratios. The boom in the stock market in the mid-1980s encouraged public offerings and rights issues (i.e., the option for existing shareholders to buy newly issued shares) and has helped reduce the high debt–equity ratios. As a result of these measures, the capital structure of Korea's corporations, particularly those listed on the Korean Stock Exchange, has improved. Debt–equity ratios have improved, but are still quite high, averaging over 3 to 1 in 1990.

Although, like Mexico, Korea's stock market is larger than those of many developed markets, it still has some characteristics of an emerging market. One reason is that prior to 1992, the stock market was closed to foreign portfolio investment, with the exception of a few funds and equity-linked securities. The Korean securities industry was sheltered from international competition.

Another reason lies in the nature of local individual and institutional investors. Securities firms developed quickly, but lack the seasoning that comes with experience over several bear and bull markets, and lack sophistication in developing a fundamental basis for investing. Members of the Korean Stock Exchange have noted that their greatest policy error during the 1980s was in allowing the growth in institutional investors to fall behind that of individual investors.

The government has consciously utilized the growing stock market to help with its privatization program, which in turn has helped to further develop the capital markets. The flotation of the Korean Electric Power Company (KEPCO) in 1989 was one of a series of privatizations of large SOEs. These included Pohang Steel & Iron (POSCO), Citizens National Bank, the Korea Exchange Bank, the Small & Medium Industry Bank, the Korea Telecommunication Authority, and the Korea Monopoly Corporation. The privatization of KEPCO was done in the broad-based, popular capitalism mode of British Telecom. KEPCO offered 21 percent of its total equity to the public. The offering price was 13,000 won per share ($19.21), but for low-income applicants who held their shares for more than three years, the price was only 9,100 won ($13.38). "Ordinary" applicants (those not considered low-income) were allocated 2 percent of the shares; low-income applicants, who could sell their shares at any time, were allocated 23.4 percent; and low-income applicants holding shares for more than three years were allocated 54.6 percent. The employee stock ownership plan was allocated 20 percent.

The offering period was from May 27 to June 1, 1989. The share offer was oversubscribed. In all, there were a remarkable 6.7 million subscribers to the share offer, who paid $1.9 billion for their shares. The shares were listed in August, and rose to 22,000 won ($32.74). KEPCO is now by far the largest company in terms of market capitalization on the Korean Stock Exchange. KEPCO is considering selling additional shares through an ADR to increase its exposure and access to the international capital markets.

In order to improve Korea's competitiveness and make SOEs more efficient, the government plans to privatize most SOEs in economic infrastructure by 1998.

Malaysia: Innovations in BOT Projects Support Privatization Success

Privatization and economic liberalization have been key features of Malaysia's program to industrialize and achieve balanced growth. A notable feature of its privatization program—one of Asia's most successful—is the reliance upon BOT methods to finance infrastructure in this rapidly industrializing country.[26] Malaysia's SOE sector was created largely to redress social inequities. However, the government realized in the 1980s that SOEs were more economically harmful than socially beneficial.

Malaysia's privatization program, which has been strongly supported by Prime Minister Mahathir, has made frequent use of the stock exchange. Concerns have been expressed about the absorptive capacity of Malaysia's capital markets for privatization, but the market has consistently been able to absorb more shares than expected. Around eighty privatizations have taken place to date, including BOT privatizations of economic infrastructure. The Malaysian Airline System and the Malaysian International Shipping Corporation were privatized through public flotations in 1985 and 1986, respectively. These and other offerings were oversubscribed, reflecting the quality of the companies privatized and anticipation of improved efficiency once they came into private hands.

In 1990, the government floated 23 percent of the huge Malaysia Telecom. In 1992, it sold $1.2 billion worth of shares in Tenaga Nasional, the national electricity company. These two privatizations have contributed greatly to the increased capitalization and market turnover of the Malaysian stock market.

In addition, Malaysia has been an innovator in the field of BOT infrastructure privatizations, and has made BOT techniques a major part of its privatization strategy. The government has approved several billion dollars worth of BOT projects, including the North–South Expressway. The government has conducted competitive tenders to invite private sector firms to participate on a BOO/BOT basis in mass urban transport, the power and gas industries, water, sewerage, and industrial waste treatment. This process will create new economic infrastructure which will be financed by the private sector.

In the power sector, for example, Malaysia has an installed generating capacity of 7,403 megawatts. By the year 2020, by which time Malaysia plans to be an industrialized economy, the country will require a total generating capacity of about 40,000 megawatts. Tenaga Nasional can create some of the additional capacity itself, but the government plans to use independent power projects under BOT arrangements to generate and sell electricity to the national grid. Five independent power project licenses were granted in 1994.[27]

Thailand: Looking to Privatization for Economic Infrastructure and Capital Market Development to Sustain Economic Growth

Due in part to underdeveloped capital markets, Thailand has yet to reap the full benefits of recent high rates of economic growth. Thailand's economy and stock market have grown quickly during the last decade.[28] From 1985 through 1994, stock market capitalization increased from $1.9 billion to $131 billion, trading value from $600 million to $80 billion, and the number of listed companies from 100 to 389.

At the same time, Thailand must further increase the breadth and depth of its shareholding base. Thailand had fewer than 400,000 shareholders at the end of 1990, less than 1 percent of the total population. This is a small number by any standards, and a fraction of the percentage one finds in developed economies. This could change over the next few years, however, now that the Securities Exchange of Thailand (SET) is encouraging securities firms to set up provincial offices. Until recently, their offices were concentrated in Bangkok. Thailand's institutional investors are also underdeveloped. This is significant, because growth in the number of individual shareholders should ideally be balanced with growth in institutional shareholding in order to provide for the professional management of financial assets.

A broad-based flotation of some of Thailand's leading SOEs would be a means not only of achieving the benefits of privatization, but also of broadening and deepening the stock market, which would distribute share ownership in Thailand, provide quality companies for the exchange, and help to achieve the government's ultimate goal of making the SET a "regional" exchange.

The Ministry of Finance of Thailand wholly or partly controls some sixty SOEs. These firms are a diverse group spread across seven sectors, but they dominate the economic infrastructure sectors—energy, transport, telecommunications, and electricity. The large and generally profitable SOEs in Thailand, such as the Electricity Generating Authority of Thailand (EGAT) and the Telephone Organization of Thailand (TOT), have not been able to keep pace with Thailand's dynamic economic growth. The Ministry of Finance plans to attract private sector finance to these SOEs rather than continue their dependence on the government's budget for capital outlays.

For the largest SOEs, the most compelling reason for privatizing by accessing the equity market is to increase access to capital. Lack of access to adequate capital sources has slowed the growth of the large, capital-intensive SOEs, such as EGAT, which are faced with rapidly expanding demand. These SOEs also have high debt–equity ratios and need to strengthen their balance sheets. It would be beneficial for all parties—the government, the SOEs, Thailand's equity market, and Thai citizens—for the SOEs to tap Thailand's stock market and begin to privatize these SOEs through share sales. However, vested interests run deep, the SOE bureaucracy is powerful, and progress has been limited.

One SOE, Thai International, the leading airline, was partially privatized in 1992. One hundred million shares, representing about 7.8 percent of the total shares, were sold, raising about $230 million. However, by pricing the shares too high, the Thai government missed an opportunity to use the broad-based model, expand share ownership and create a broader constituency for privatization.

Thailand has been a leader in the promotion of BOT privatizations, although actually coming to closure on such transactions is proving more difficult than expected. In addition to the Bangkok Second Stage Expressway, the government has approved two other mass transit BOT projects worth several billion dollars for Bangkok. It has also approved a $6 billion telecommunications BOT project to provide 3 million new telephone lines, and plans to install an additional 1.1 million telephone lines to meet forecast demand. Instead of making any further investment in plants to produce more electricity, EGAT intends to invite the private sector to make the necessary investment and then sell the electricity back to EGAT for onward distribution to the public.[29]

Some of the private sector companies awarded BOT contracts are raising equity finance. TT&T, which has a BOT contract to install one million telephone lines in Thai provinces, launched its issue in 1994 with a domestic and an international tranche totaling $290 million. TelecomAsia, another BOT company, sold over $1 billion in 1993, half to domestic investors and half to overseas institutions. It is the second largest company in terms of capitalization on the SET. [30]

Sri Lanka: Deregulation and Privatization Spur Stock Market's Take-Off

Sri Lanka, one of the smaller emerging markets, experienced a "take-off," with market capitalization growing from $300 million to $2 billion during the period of 1990 to 1992.[31]

Public share trading first began in July 1984 and was based on the "open outcry" system. Manual, paper-based operations on the Colombo Stock Exchange (CSE) were slow and cumbersome, which limited the efficiency and timeliness of share transfers. Even before the increase in trading following the "emergence" of Sri Lanka, the CSE was experiencing clearing and settlement difficulties.

Other problems were structural in nature. Many Sri Lankan companies were unwilling to list on the CSE, which limited the supply of shares on the market and reduced liquidity. Tax policies encouraged companies to favor debt over equity financing. Most of the companies which did list did not trade actively, and there was little trading in the market. None of the brokers operated outside Colombo, and the services they provided to clients were limited. Investment research and portfolio management skills were virtually non-existent.

The demand for shares was also severely limited. The Sri Lankan public was generally unaware of the potential benefits of investing in shares. If aware, people frequently lacked confidence in the market, and tended to prefer less risky, albeit lower-yielding, bank deposits. Institutional investors, which should have been a significant source of demand, were typically government owned and served as captives for low-yielding government bonds. Foreign portfolio investment was effectively eliminated by a 100 percent tax on purchased shares.

But Sri Lanka demonstrates how quickly things can turn around for an emerging market. Since June 1990, the CSE has demonstrated a remarkable increase in market capitalization, turnover, price index, and valuation. The CSE has become an attractive destination for emerging market fund managers, as well as Sri Lankan investors.

The government's decision to abolish the 100 percent tax on foreign purchase of Sri Lankan shares in June 1990, and to allow foreign investors to remit their sale proceeds out of Sri Lanka was key to this takeoff. Foreign participation was critical in correcting the undervaluation of the market at that time. The government of Sri Lanka has taken specific actions to develop the stock market, including needed legal and regulatory changes, an improvement in exchange operations, additional efforts to increase the supply and demand for shares, a public awareness program to inform citizens of the benefits of share investing, and a privatization program featuring broad-based share sales.

Sri Lanka's financial institutions are relatively diverse. They are capable of providing private borrowers with, at least, short-term working capital. A host of policy and institutional problems, however, make longer-term financing from local Sri Lankan sources virtually impossible. Some interest rates are controlled, and the use of market-based monetary instruments is limited. The development of Sri Lanka's financial institutions is also impeded by serious debt-recovery problems, insufficiently rigorous central bank supervision, and inadequate accounting and auditing.

Sri Lanka has sold forty-two SOEs to the private sector since embarking on its privatization program. Sri Lanka's privatization strategy, known as the "60-30-10" approach, has enabled it to achieve broad-based shareholding and also the related objectives of finding core investors, obtaining increased foreign investment, and ensuring employee participation. In chronological order, 60 percent (i.e., majority shareholding) of the corporatized SOEs shares are sold by a tender process to an investor (usually foreign) who can provide the resources to make the enterprise more competitive. Then 30 percent is offered to the public in a public share offer and 10 percent is given to the company employees. (The actual percentages can vary somewhat depending on the enterprise.)

The strategy has several features that merit consideration by other countries. Selling 60 percent to a foreign investor helps provide new management, technology, access to markets, and financing, and the majority shareholding ensures that the investor will have sufficient interest to make the company work. Selling 30 percent to the public helps to supply much needed shares on the market, the lack of which had constrained the development of Sri Lanka's stock market. A 30 percent local holding also serves as a check on the foreign investor by requiring that the company issue annual reports and hold public stockholder meetings. Finally, 10 percent of the shares are given to the employees, out of concern for fairness and the low prevailing wages in the country. Employee participation also helps to turn what is normally a group opposed to privatization into a supporter.

As Sri Lanka's program advances, the government of Sri Lanka has developed an alternative "fast-track" privatization approach. It simply lists companies in which it has majority ownership. It then offers to sell a block of at least 51 percent of the shares through a share broker to competing corporate investors. The winner is the highest bidder for the block of shares. It is relatively simple and very transparent. The remainder of the shares are disposed of in smaller blocks of shares through the secondary market, to the general public, and by transfer to employees.

The impact is essentially the same as the 60-30-10 strategy, in terms of creating core investors, attracting new resources, and later broad-basing a minority portion of shares and including employee participation. This fast-track method avoids some of the lengthy procedural difficulties (marketing, tendering, evaluation, and transparency) that had been encountered in selling the majority shareholding block using the 60-30-10 approach.

The privatization program seems to have had a demonstration effect for private sector companies. In 1994, more than a dozen IPOs came to the market, increasing the market's capitalization and liquidity.

Sri Lanka has also established a BOO/BOT privatization program, which, though delayed by elections, has the potential to enable the private sector to provide needed economic infrastructure to enable Sri Lanka to reach its goal of becoming a newly industrializing country (NIC) early in the next century.

NOTES

1. Sources include Sunita Kikeri, John Nellis, and Mary Shirley, *Privatization: The Lessons of Experience* (Washington, D.C.: The World Bank, 1992); Christopher Adam, William Cavendish, and Percy S. Mistry, *Adjusting Privatization: Case Studies from Developing Countries* (London: James Currey Ltd., 1992); and author's estimates.

2. This section on the United Kingdom draws on John Redwood, *Popular Capitalism* (London: Routledge, 1988) and Oliver Letwin, *Privatising the World* (London: Cassell, 1988).

3. Alexander Marquardt and Ellen H. Clarke, "French Privatizations and International Capital Markets," *Northwestern Journal of International Law & Business,* 15 (1994): 408, 411.

4. Ibid, 408.

5. This section draws on Organization of Economic Co-operation and Development, *Financial Market Trends* (Paris: OECD, 1995), 21–27.

6. Ibid., 21–23.

7. Ibid.

8. World Bank, *Argentina's Privatization Program: Experience, Issues, and Lessons* (Washington, D.C.: The World Bank, 1993), 16.

9. Privatisation International, *Privatisation Yearbook 1995* (London: Privatisation International, 1995), 188.

10. Marjorie T. Stanley, *The Irwin Guide to Investing in Emerging Markets* (Chicago: Irwin, 1995), 135–145.

11. World Bank, *Argentina's Privatization Program*, 14.

12. International Finance Corporation, *Emerging Stock Markets Factbook* (Washington, D.C.: The International Finance Corporation, 1995); and World Bank, "Argentina: Capital Markets Study," a report prepared by the World Bank, Washington, D.C., 1994.

13. Stanley, *The Irwin Guide*, 136.

14. Keith K. H. Park and Antoine van Agtmael, eds., *The World's Emerging Stock Markets* (Chicago: Probus, 1992), 335.

15. Toso, Roberto, "The Chilean Privatization Experience," a paper prepared for Harvard University, The Center for International Affairs, Cambridge, Mass., 1990.

16. Stanley, *The Irwin Guide*, 123–124.

17. Privatisation International, *Privatisation Yearbook 1995*, 208.

18. World Bank, *Trends in Developing Economies* (Washington, D.C.: The World Bank, 1995), 347.

19. Stanley, *The Irwin Guide*, 390.

20. World Bank, *Trends in Developing Economies*, 348.

21. Privatisation International, *Privatisation Yearbook 1995*, 218.

22. This section draws on Michael P. McLindon, "Macroeconomic Aspects of Privatization: The Case of Jamaica" (Paper presented at the Seminar on Privatization Strategies and Techniques for Development, Center for Privatization, Washington, D.C., 1988). See also Roger Leeds, "Privatization in Jamaica: Two Case Studies," Cambridge, Mass.: Harvard University Center for Business and Government, 1987.

23. Risk Publications, *Emerging Markets Investor Factbook* (London: Risk Publications, 1995), 57–58.

24. Privatisation International, *Privatisation Yearbook 1995*, 176.

25. This section on Korea draws on an unpublished working paper by the author, and Michael P. McLindon and Richard Samuelson, "Korea 1992: Foreign Perspective," *Business Korea* (July 1990).

26. This section draws on Matthew L. Hensley and Edward White, "The Privatization Experience in Malaysia," *Columbia Journal of World Business*, 28, no. 1 (1993).

27. Privatisation Interntional, *Privatisation Yearbook*, 176.

28. This section draws on Michael P. McLindon, Richard Downer, Richard Samuelson, David Levintow, and David Smith, "Privatization in Thailand," a report prepared for the Center for Privatization, Washington, D.C., 1990.

29. Privatisation International, *Privatisation Yearbook 1995*, 287.

30. IFC, *Emerging Stock Markets Factbook*.

31. This section draws on McLindon, Samuelson, Page, and Shiner, "Sri Lanka," in *The World's Emerging Stock Markets*, edited by K. H. Park and Antoine van Agtmael (Chicago: Probus, 1992).

CHAPTER SIX

MASS PRIVATIZATION AND CAPITAL MARKETS

Eastern Europe and the Former Soviet Union

In 1989, world history was made. As the twentieth century approached its final decade, the Berlin Wall fell and Eastern Europe achieved its independence from the Soviet Union. In 1991, the Soviet Union disintegrated, spawning fifteen newly independent states, of which Russia was largest in size, population, and resources. The command economies had imploded.

After the celebrations, policymakers in these countries faced the challenge of restructuring and modernizing their economies. The dead hand of bureaucracy in these command economies was ubiquitous. SOEs dominated the economies of Eastern Europe and the former Soviet Union. There were 25,000 large and medium SOEs in Russia, 8,500 in Poland, 6,000 in the Czech and Slovak Federal Republic, 2,400 in Lithuania, and over 1,200 in Moldova.[1]

Under a planned economy, SOE managers had no incentives to make products that consumers wanted, much less to make profits or reduce costs. SOEs remitted any profits to the state budget, and the budget and bank "loans" covered losses by other SOEs, which faced no effective budget constraint. The banks were passive conduits of finance between central planners and the SOEs.

How could these countries rebuild their economies to realize the opportunities presented by political freedom? This chapter discusses why it was necessary to develop mass privatization techniques in the transition economies of Eastern Europe and the former Soviet Union. It reviews different approaches to mass privatization, and concludes that the use of privatization certificates, commonly referred to as vouchers, is the most effective. The techniques of mass privatization by vouchers are explained. The experiences of mass privatization and capital market development in the Czech and Slovak Federal Republic, Russia, and Moldova are reviewed. Finally, it is noted that capital market development is more advanced in some countries adopting mass privatization by voucher than in countries which have opted for other approaches to privatization.

MASS PRIVATIZATION

Owing to the dominance of the state and SOEs, privatization was the sine qua non for restructuring the command economies. But what kind of privatization? As discussed in Chapter 5, privatization by public share sale can be appropriate for blue-chip SOEs, especially when revenue is important to the government. It can also serve as a model to encourage private sector firms to sell shares publicly. However, this method is too slow for countries with a large number of SOEs, most of which are in mediocre or worse shape and require restructuring. Case-by-case sale of shares requires expensive skills and complex procedures to prepare enterprises for sale. Any attempt to restructure the hundreds and thousands of SOEs before privatization would overwhelm the political system; bureaucrats with vested interests would be able to interfere at every turn. In addition, citizens require some money in order to participate in privatization share sales. But in the Czech and Slovak Federal Republic, for example, total private savings amounted to only a small percent of the book value of the enterprises to be privatized.

A new type of privatization was required. Groups of enterprises had to be transferred quickly to the population, using standard, transparent procedures. This approach to privatization has come to be called mass privatization. Despite intense initial skepticism, the experience of mass privatization in countries in Eastern Europe and the former Soviet Union, notably the Czech and Slovak Federal Republic, Russia, Lithuania Moldova, and Kyrgyzstan, has demonstrated that it is indeed possible to privatize thousands of enterprises within one to two years, or even faster.

Mass privatization defers, until after privatization, the need for time-consuming and expensive elements required for a public share sale, such as accounting adjustments and market-based valuations. Mass privatization with vouchers allows every citizen to participate, and gives them a stake in economic reform by making them shareholders. Mass privatization can be an engine to develop capital markets.

The issue of revenue is important for countries considering privatization, especially in countries with stock markets that can raise large proceeds from privatization. Governments must consider the fact that mass privatization does not generate revenue. (Some governments charge a fee for vouchers, to cover administrative costs.) However, the speed of mass privatization enables restructuring of enterprises to begin much more quickly. Reduced losses by SOEs and increased tax revenue from restructured SOEs after privatization can be substantial, although these gains are difficult to calculate ex ante.

Types of Mass Privatization

Experiences in Eastern Europe and the former Soviet Union have yielded three basic models of mass privatization:

- "Rapid" case-by-case—the former German Democratic Republic (East Germany).
- Mass privatization through intermediary mutual funds—Poland and Kazakhstan.
- Voucher mass privatization—The Czech and Slovak Federal Republic, Russia, Lithuania, Moldova, and Kyrgyzstan.

The first model has been successful, but is unlikely to be replicated. In the former German Democratic Republic, a well-financed and powerful implementing agency, the Treuhandanstalt, privatized over 14,500 medium and large SOEs through case-by-case trade sales, primarily to West German companies. This notable achievement, though, is unique owing to the special circumstances of the former East Germany's integration into the prosperous Federal Republic of Germany, and especially the latter's willingness to spend huge sums of money to make it work.

The second model of mass privatization, through intermediary investment (or mutual) funds exclusively, has not been effectively implemented in any country. One reasons for the failure seems to lie in the fact that the governments try to organize and implicitly control the investment funds, rather than allow them to be created independently by the private sector. Another reason is that the exclusive use of intermediary investment funds denies the citizen the right to exercise his or her voucher to bid directly for shares in a particular SOE.

Mass privatization through vouchers, the third model, has proven to be a notable success if the right techniques are used. This type of mass privatization has also permitted capital markets to emerge where virtually none had existed before.

Mass privatization has been confined to former command economies. Yet there are many other countries in which the government owns hundreds and even thousands of SOEs. Mass privatization techniques can be adapted for use in virtually any country to speed up privatization programs and create a capital market with a broad base of citizen shareholders.

Issues and Techniques in
Mass Privatization by Vouchers

The essence of mass privatization is to create a speedy, streamlined process to transfer groups of SOEs to the private sector, so that restructuring of SOEs can begin and capital markets can develop.[2]

Voucher Design: Creating the Demand for Mass Privatization A voucher is simply a piece of paper (albeit with special safety features to deter counterfeiting) distributed to eligible citizens, which enables them to participate in voucher auctions for the shares of enterprises in the mass privatization program. Vouchers may also come in the form of dematerialized privatization accounts, opened for the benefit of citizens at banks or other institutions. However, experience suggests that paper vouchers are better because they are tangible and more readily understood by citizens. It is also more difficult for bureaucrats to slow down or stop privatization once citizens have vouchers in their hands.

Some countries have distributed vouchers to all citizens over eighteen years of age. Others have made everyone, regardless of age, eligible to receive vouchers, with parents making the decisions for children. Some distribute vouchers free of charge, while others charge a small fee to cover administrative costs.

A voucher is often the first security owned by a citizen. As noted, experience points to the importance of letting citizens decide how to use their vouchers, rather than requiring them to work exclusively through investment (or mutual) funds. Citizens should still have the right to assign their voucher to an investment fund if not inclined to use it themselves, as was the case, for example, in the Czech and Slovak Federal Republic, Russia, Lithuania, Moldova, and Kyrgyzstan.

A voucher can be tradable or non-tradable. Programs in which the voucher was non-tradable, such as in the Czech and Slovak Federal Republic and Moldova, have been successful. However, experience from Russia and Kyrgyzstan indicates that a tradable voucher has attractive benefits for the development of capital markets and post-privatization enterprise restructuring. Tradable vouchers help brokers and dealers and investment funds before mass privatization begins: They allow these future capital markets agents to gain needed experience in trade transactions, and to earn income. Trading vouchers before and during mass privatization anticipates the trading of shares of the privatized enterprises. A tradable voucher also encourages the emergence of core investors who buy blocks of vouchers before the national auctions take place. These core investors will own, manage and restructure the newly privatized enterprises. A tradable voucher is also more practical for processing auction results. Processing auction results with a small number of large investors is easier than a large number of small investors.

Vouchers can come in different forms. Some countries have given citizens variable bidding power in their vouchers depending on years of employment, for example, or salary level. Experience indicates that the simplest type of voucher is one which can be used one time at one auction for one enterprise (or, alternatively, assigned to an investment fund). This arrangement reduces the number of processing transactions required, reduces errors, and speeds up the program.

Another issue in voucher design is whether vouchers should be assigned any nominal "value," or simply be denominated in investment "points." Russia gave its vouchers a nominal value of 10,000 rubles, and the program worked well. However, on balance, a point system, as used in the Czech and Slovak Federal Republic, Moldova, and Kyrgyzstan, is more logical. Denominating vouchers in local currency has two pitfalls. First, if vouchers are tradable, citizens may feel cheated if market trading values fall below the nominal value of the vouchers. Second, citizens may be confused if they have such vouchers and enter the auction process to bid for shares. They may feel that the value of the shares they receive must somehow be related to the nominal value of the vouchers. A point system is more in keeping with the spirit of mass privatization. Mass privatization rests, in part, on the principle that determining the value of shares in SOEs is an exercise best carried out by the capital markets after privatization, and not by governments before privatization.

Enterprise Preparation: Creating the Supply of SOEs for Mass Privatization Mass privatization requires a quick, streamlined, decentralized process, with deadlines to ensure a steady supply of SOEs to the mass privatization auctions.

A simplified Privatization Package, comprised of the corporatization document and privatization plan, can be mailed to each SOE that will participate in the mass privatization program. The SOE would be allowed about two months to complete and return the forms to the Ministry of Privatization (or other agency responsible for mass privatization). One week after receipt of the Privatization Package, the ministry would add the firm to the list of those scheduled for auction. If deadlines are not met by the firms, the ministry itself could fill out the forms based on available information, and enter the companies onto the auction lists.

Mass privatization first requires the conversion of the SOE into a joint-stock company, a process known as corporatization. Corporatization enables the enterprise to issue shares, which are initially 100-percent owned by the government. Corporatization typically determines the number of shares and the initial value of the company. After corporatization, the former SOE is no longer an adjunct to the branch ministry. An important consideration in the establishment of joint-stock companies via corporatization is to create *open* joint-stock companies, so that company shares can be traded without undue restrictions.

It is critical in the corporatization phase of mass privatization to avoid lengthy, complex valuations. The simplest way is to use the most recently available book value as the company valuation. Nevertheless, some governments require new valuations for corporatization, often using complex indices to adjust for inflation. This takes time and uses scarce resources, and has not been shown to add much useful information.

It is the task of the capital market, not the government, to make judgements about future cash flows and their attendant risk, an analysis that is the best means of valuing a company and which is best carried out after privatization. Some may insist on restating the financial accounts, in order to present a more meaningful disclosure on the SOE. However, improvements in the financial accounts of an individual enterprise, and accounting standards in general, are also tasks that belong to the larger effort of post-privatization restructuring, a process which capital markets will tend to hasten, given their need for reliable information. A transformation or restatement of the accounts before privatization is not worth the effort.

Preparation of the corporatization document and the privatization plan should be decentralized, with the enterprises themselves undertaking most of the work. The privatization plan presents information in a highly simplified form for citizens to review at the national auction centers, including the name, location, and industry in which the enterprise operates. Financial information provided should be based on what is available, stated in summary form to highlight key items from the income statement and balance sheet. While no great credence can be given to the accuracy of this information, it should afford bidders a rough and ready yardstick for comparing enterprises put up for auction. (For example, a firm with higher profit than another may attract more vouchers.) Any errors in information can be corrected at the bid collection sites. This approach would help to assure a steady stream of enterprises ready for auction and handing over to private owners, which would mean that restructuring could begin sooner.

Preferential share distribution, or the allocation of shares to workers and managers, commences after corporatization but before public auctions. Shares may be allocated to workers and managers free of charge, at a nominal cost, for vouchers, or some combination thereof. The preferential share distribution is made out of a sense of fairness to those who have worked in the enterprise, and also to act as an incentive for workers and managers to support and speed up privatization. The percentage of shares set aside has varied greatly, depending on the power of the workers and managers. Workers and managers in the Czech and Slovak Federal Republic generally received less than 10 percent of the shares; in Moldova, 20 percent; while in Russia, most workers and managers received 51 percent.

Auction Techniques: Unpriced Bids The lessons of the Czech and Slovak Federal Republic, Russia, and Kyrgyzstan point to the use of "unpriced bids" as the most efficient auction method. (The term auction as used here should not be confused with an open outcry auction. It refers to a "subscription for shares" auction; that is, the process of filling out an application form to "bid" for shares with vouchers.)

In the Czech and Slovak Federal Republic, the use of a repricing and reauctioning mechanism for oversubscriptions (discussed in more detail later) required that some enterprises be offered in five successive auctions before they were finally privatized. Russians had two bidding options: one which was similar to the Czech Republic's reprice and reauction, and another which utilized "unpriced bids." The Russian experience shows that unpriced bids were more popular and procedurally less complex than the Czech reprice and reauction or other bidding procedures. Kyrgyzstan used unpriced bids only, which proved to be simple and successful.

In an unpriced bid, the number of shares in an individual enterprise awarded to citizens depends upon the numbers of vouchers bid for the shares of that enterprise. For example, if 50 vouchers are bid (by individuals, investment funds, or both) for a company with 100 shares available, then each voucher is awarded two shares. In the case where the number of vouchers bid exceeds the number of shares available, stock splits would be used to increase the number of shares available. For example, if 200 vouchers bid for a company with 100 shares, then the company would effect a 2 for 1 stock split and each voucher would receive one share. Depending on the particular numbers of shares offered in voucher auctions and the number of vouchers bid, computer algorithms can be developed to determine the optimal stock split. (Stock splits have no economic meaning—they do not lessen the value of the enterprise, although they reduce the ownership claim of each voucher in proportion to the demand for the shares.)

This method of share allocation helps to prevent vouchers from being bid exclusively on the good companies that are being put up for auction. If many vouchers are bid on just the good companies, then everyone's ownership claim will be relatively small. This points to the possibility of saving some vouchers to bid on second- and third-tier SOEs in the mass privatization program, because relatively larger ownership stakes can be won for fewer vouchers. Thus, there is a built-in incentive for individuals, and especially investment funds, to spread out their voucher bids in rough proportion to the perceived value of the SOEs that are being auctioned.

Privatization using unpriced bids is quick and efficient: Each enterprise is only auctioned once, and citizens are assured of receiving shares if they bid their vouchers. Privatization is rapid, allowing restructuring and capital markets activities to begin.

Linking Mass Privatization with Capital Markets The most successful form of mass privatization, the voucher method, has also been the most useful for creating capital markets. A secondary capital market is a logical corollary to mass privatization, and critical if citizens are to benefit as new shareholders. Privatized enterprises and other newly created enterprises will have to attract new capital to finance restructuring and growth. The banking system can supply some of this capital (especially if the banks are privatized and restructured), but the primary equity market will have to take the financial lead.

The links between capital market development and mass privatization are particularly important:[3]

- Capital markets create a liquid market in which the newly created shareholders and intermediaries can buy and sell shares. Except when the vouchers are tradable, this opportunity to buy and sell shares will be the first tangible benefit for citizens of the country.
- Capital markets can play a critical role in providing corporate governance to the newly privatized SOEs.
- Capital markets play a key role in the post-privatization restructuring of enterprises. Since most managers and employees in former Soviet Union countries are shareholders in the enterprises where they work, the capital markets will provide them with an important incentive to restructure. Through changes in stock prices, and therefore company valuations, the stock exchanges hold up a carrot for companies which restructure and perform well, and a stick for those which perform poorly.
- Capital markets allow ownership and capital structure to change over time and serve as a vehicle for foreign direct and portfolio investment.
- As capital markets develop further, companies are able to issue new shares to raise equity capital to finance expansion and modernization, and avoid an excessive reliance on debt capital.

THE CZECH AND SLOVAK FEDERAL REPUBLIC

Until the revolution of 1989, Czechoslovakia, with its hardline Communist government, was a staunch adherent of a planned economy. Despite this, the Czech and Slovak Federal Republic embarked on some of the most dramatic market reforms in the region following the changes of 1989.[4]

After careful planning, the Czech and Slovak mass privatization through vouchers began in June 1992. Citizens over eighteen years of age could participate by registering to join the program and paying a fee of about $35, equivalent to a week's average take-home pay, for mass privatization vouchers in the form of bidding "points." These points could be used to bid for stock priced in terms of shares per 100 investment points. Individuals could use their vouchers to bid directly for the shares in a company. A participant bid for shares by specifying the enterprise's code on the coupon and handing it in to a registration center (usually a post office).

Individuals could also ask an Investment Privatization Fund to manage their vouchers for them in order to diversify risk and permit professional management of the shares. The nascent private sector responded by creating more than 400 investment funds. The investment funds, which were legally established as joint-stock companies, operated like open-ended mutual funds investing in shares on behalf of individuals. An individual investment fund was restricted from holding more than 20 percent of the shares of any enterprise.

A list was published of all companies whose shares were to be offered in the mass privatization program. All shares carried the same "price" (three shares per 100 points) in the first round of bidding. Individuals and investment funds were given about two weeks to register their bids, after which all the bids were tallied. If demand for the shares of a particular enterprise equaled or fell short of supply, then the shares were allotted to the bidders at the price for the round and any remaining shares carried over to the next round of bidding. If total demand for a given company's shares exceeded supply by less than 25 percent and bids by individuals were less than the total number of shares offered, then all shares were allocated by first satisfying all individual bids and then distributing the remainder to investment funds by cutting their bids pro-rata. In all cases in which the demand exceeded supply by more than 25 percent, the entire offer was carried over to the next round of bidding without any allotment of shares in that round.

The shares carried over from the previous round of bidding were re-offered in the next round after repricing the shares (in terms of points per share) according to the degree of excess demand. The bidding and allocation was done according to the principles of round one. The rounds of bidding were repeated until all shares were sold.

The experience of the Czech and Slovak Federal Republic points to one of the key lessons learned: the reprice and reauction method adopted was unnecessarily complicated, giving rise to the simpler system of "unpriced bids," used in Russia. It has been argued that the determination of the "price" of the shares should be left to the capital markets after privatization. The purpose of the privatization is to transfer those shares to the private sector as quickly as possible.

Results of Mass Privatization

In the first round of the Czech and Slovak mass privatization program, 8.5 million citizens (out of a population of 15.5 million) bid for shares in 1,491 enterprises with a book value of approximately $10.7 billion. Two-thirds of the citizens placed their vouchers with the funds. Shafik notes that the entire cycle of project preparation, public information, and nationwide bidding took fifteen months—an average of over three medium- and large-scale enterprises privatized per *day*.[5] As noted in chapter 2, other developing countries have averaged three privatizations a year since 1980. The average value of shares purchased by citizens, who spent $35 each to buy voucher booklets, was $1,000 by 1994.[6]

The Czech and Slovak Federal Republic underwent its "velvet divorce" on January 1, 1993. The Czech Republic undertook a second wave of voucher auctions, which was completed in November 1994. An additional 861 companies were privatized via vouchers to 6.2 million Czech citizens.

A recent study by Lieberman and his colleagues of mass privatization programs made the following evaluation of the program:

There is no question that the mass privatization program has been a great success. In the Czech Republic alone it has led to the privatization of 70 to 80 percent of state-owned enterprises in a variety of sectors—industry, construction, agro-processing, and banking. . . . It has decentralized the problem of restructuring Czech industry and has placed it in the hands of new private owners, rather than the hands of government. It has been sequenced well into an overall program of reforms, so that today the Czech economy has been largely reformed and liberalized.[7]

Capital Market Development

The mass privatization plan has served as a catalyst to the stock markets in the Czech and Slovak Republics. The original mass privatization plan succeeded in its goal of creating about 8.5 million shareholders in both republics. The spontaneous emergence of more than 400 voucher funds boosted public awareness and interest through extensive advertising.

The Prague Stock Exchange reopened in April 1993. (Trading was suspended at the stock exchange in Prague in 1938, and remained so after World War II. The Exchange was officially abolished in 1952.)[8] For 1994, the IFC reports that there were 1,024 listed companies on the Prague Stock Exchange, representing $12.6 billion in market capitalization. The vast majority of those companies were those that had been a part of the mass privatization program. Another exchange, RM-S (an over-the-counter system), was brought into operation at the same time. Its primary objective was to provide greater capital market accessibility. Four hundred RM-S outlets have been established, allowing individuals to trade directly or through professional brokers.

RUSSIA

After the overthrow of the Communist Party in 1991, Russia chose mass privatization to depoliticize the economy, create real property rights, quickly transfer SOEs to the private sector so that restructuring could begin, and develop domestic capital markets to help to finance restructuring and growth.[9] A key goal was to build popular support for the reform program through widespread distribution of shares in SOEs to Russian citizens.

Mass Privatization

As the first step of Russia's mass privatization program, about half of Russian state-owned enterprises were corporatized; that is, turned into joint-stock companies. Workers and managers were given three options for share ownership in the firms that were a part of the mass privatization program. Most chose Option 2, which allowed managers and workers, together, to buy 51 percent of the voting shares at a low price (for cash, vouchers, or the retained earnings of the firm). Although this was a very high percentage, it was deemed a necessary price to pay for the critical support of workers and managers in the mass privatization program. Workers and managers owned their shares as individuals (rather than as collectives), and were free to sell their shares at any time.

Freely tradable vouchers were distributed to 144 million Russians. The national voucher-auction system was established in more than eighty-five regions, with 750 bid-collection centers. Russian citizens were given several bidding options. By far the most popular was the "unpriced bid" method. It provided a simple means to process auction results and award shares. Every citizen was guaranteed to receive shares under this method.

As with the Czech program, investment funds played a prominent role. Approximately 650 investment funds were created. Owned and operated by the private sector, these investment funds openly competed with each other for the right to manage citizens' vouchers.

As a result of the mass privatization voucher program, about 14,000 medium- and large-scale enterprises have been privatized. An estimated 40 million Russians are now shareholders. Tens of thousands of small-scale enterprises have also been privatized through open outcry auctions.

Capital Markets

The challenge in developing capital markets is much greater in Russia than in the Czech Republic. This is due to the enormous size of Russia, and the fact that it was under Communist control for three decades longer than the Czech Republic. Although there have been some notable reformers in Russia, the overall political support for economic and market reforms is not as strong as in the Czech Republic.

Russia's mass privatization program has produced thousands of privatized companies whose tradable shares serve as a basis for capital markets. According to the IFC, by the end of 1994, there were 200 listed companies with a market capitalization of $30 billion. Many other companies trade in several regional over-the-counter markets. The challenge will be to develop the institutions, laws, regulations, and physical infrastructure to enable the capital markets to assist restructuring and facilitate productive investment in the economy. This task is made more difficult by the fact that the Russian Parliament is often dominated by Communist sentiment, which is hostile to a market economy.

Fortunately, Russia has made a start in developing its secondary and primary markets. In Russia, citizens are free to trade their vouchers, which was not the case in the Czech and Slovak Republic. This arrangement created a large secondary trading market for vouchers. Vouchers were a security which helped emerging broker–dealer networks to gain trading experience and generate revenue. Tradable vouchers enabled citizens to realize an immediate cash benefit from the program.

In Russia, economic growth and the survival of enterprises will depend upon attracting new capital to finance restructuring and modernization. The stock market will influence restructuring. Shareholders, managers, and workers have a critical incentive to make the enterprises more productive and efficient, since they would be the primary beneficiaries of the rise in share price that attends an improvement in productivity. A well-functioning secondary market, will in turn, provide confidence to potential investors and the privatized enterprises to raise new equity capital. The secondary market will also give individual and institutional investors the confidence that a fair, efficient, and liquid market will be available once they decide to sell their shares later.

The immediate challenge for capital market development in Russia is to create a functioning secondary market. Basic capital markets infrastructure (registrars and transfer agents, secondary markets, shareholder voting, and dividend payment arrangements) is needed for citizens to realize their rights as shareholders. A functioning primary market must also be created, to enable privatized enterprises and newly created companies to expand their capital base in order to restructure and modernize.

MOLDOVA

The centerpiece of Moldova's economic reform program has been its mass privatization program.[10] Efforts to begin the mass privatization program began in earnest in January 1994. A technical assistance team of over 100 people, managed by the author of this book, played an instrumental role in the successful launching of the program, in cooperation with the Ministry of Privatization. Assistance was first provided to the government in distributing vouchers. This was accomplished through an open tender to hire Moldovan private sector firms.

Once the February elections of 1994 and the reorganization of Moldova's government by the Agrarian party were concluded, the government was able to make mass privatization a priority. In March and April, the technical assistance team helped the government draft the required legislation to implement the Privatization Law, and redesigned the auction procedures to speed up the program. Moldova moved quickly to implement the program under the new Ministry of Privatization, created in March 1994, and the leadership of its Minister, Ceslav Ciobanu, an economist and presidential advisor.

Field visits were made to identify a good candidate enterprise for the first pilot auction. A pilot auction is important because it enables the bugs in the system— procedures, processing, software—to be worked out. A low-profile candidate, preferably located outside of the capital city and in which workers and management support privatization of the enterprise, is an ideal candidate for a pilot auction. Thus, a beer factory in Orhei, a small town about an hour's drive from the capital of Chisinau, was identified as a good candidate to initiate the mass privatization program.

In early June 1994, more than 400 people were trained to operate bid-collection sites throughout Moldova. By June, the first pilot auction of the beer factory had taken place, and the rollout of the mass privatization began the following month. Throughout Moldova, 115 bid-collection sites were established. In Chisinau, the Ministry established a national center to collect applications and process auction results. After three additional successful auctions, the mass privatization infrastructure was firmly in place by October 1994. By the latter part of 1995, the mass privatization program was completed, having achieved the privatization of 1,132 medium and large enterprises and 613 small-scale enterprises. The newly privatized enterprises represent two-thirds of Moldova's industrial base.

The mass privatization program has created the beginnings of a capital market. More than 3.5 million of Moldova's 4.5 million citizens are shareholders. As noted in Chapter 4, the Moldovan mass privatization program sought to privatize the process of privatization as much as possible, to help the nascent private sector acquire the skills and experience to become capital markets agents. By the end of the mass privatization program, forty-three investment funds, eleven trust companies, fifty-eight broker-dealers, and thirty independent-share registrars had gone into business.

A second, complementary capital markets project was charged with developing the institutional structure for

Moldova's capital markets, primarily by establishing a computerized stock exchange and a regulatory framework. The Chisinau Stock Exchange opened in June 1995. By the end of 1995, the number of listed companies was seven, and stock market capitalization was $25 million. Stock exchange activity is expected to grow substantially in 1996.

The *Financial Times* notes that Moldova is "seen as a model of the post communism reform . . . Its clean privatization program and the creation of well-regulated capital markets are opening up opportunities for foreign investors . . . "[11]

IMPACT OF MASS PRIVATIZATION ON CAPITAL MARKETS

The experience of the Czech and Slovak Federal Republic and Russia, which utilized mass privatization with vouchers, and Poland and Hungary, which have not, offer an opportunity to compare the impact of privatization strategy on capital market development. As Table 6.1 indicates, the number of listed companies and the extent of market capitalization are much greater in the Czech Republic and Russia than in Poland and Hungary.

Table 6.1
Capital Market Indicators

Country	Number of Companies Listed	Market Capitalization (US$ billions)
Czech Republic	1024	13.0
Russia	200	30.0
Poland	44	3.1
Hungary	40	1.6

Source: International Finance Corporation, *Emerging Stock Markets Factbook 1995* (Washington, D.C.: The International Finance Corporation, 1995).

Of course, there is more to capital market development than can be captured by any single set of numbers. As discussed in Chapter 4, there are many qualitative, institutional elements that are critical, including regulation, competition, and the development of capital markets agents and institutions. Moreover, capital market development is a process that takes years and decades. Thus, a definitive conclusion on the impact of mass privatization by vouchers cannot be made at present, although the developments to date are encouraging.

At least in the Czech Republic and Russia, and more recently, Moldova, a critical mass of privatized companies, shareholders, and investment funds has been created. These fledgling capital markets provide a powerful incentive for enterprises to restructure, and provide a means for the privatized enterprises to raise new equity finance for growth.

NOTES

1. Ira W. Lieberman, Andrew Ewing, Michal Mejstrik, Joyita Mukherjee, and Peter Fidler, eds., *Mass Privatization in Central and Eastern Europe and the Former Soviet Union: A Comparative Analysis* (Washington D.C.: The World Bank, 1995), 1. The figure for Moldova is the author's estimate.

2. This section is based on the author's advisory experience in, and field research on, mass privatization programs in the former Soviet Union, especially Moldova, and Eastern Europe. The ideas expressed here have benefitted considerably from discussions over a period of time with Walter Coles, Heather Degarmo, and William Mako, although the views expressed in this section and chapter do not necessarily reflect their views or those of their employers. It is appropriate to note the important and decisive role played by Walter Coles, the USAID NIS privatization officer, in the mass privatization and capital markets programs in Russia, Moldova, and other former Soviet Union countries.

3. Some of these points are made in Lieberman et al., *Mass Privatization*.

4. This section draws on Nemat Shafik, "Making a Market: Mass Privatization in the Czech and Slovak Republics," policy

research working paper 1231, The World Bank, Washington, D.C., 1993.

5. Ibid.

6. Neil King, "The Second Wave," *Central European Economic Review* (Spring 1994): 16.

7. Lieberman et al., *Mass Privatization*, 10.

8. Marjorie T. Stanley, *The Irwin Guide to Investing in Emerging Markets* (Chicago: Irwin, 1995), 345.

9. This section draws on Maxim Boycko, Andrei Shleifer, and Robert Vishny, *Privatizing Russia* (Cambridge, Mass.: MIT Press, 1995); and Ira W. Lieberman and John Nellis, eds., *Russia: Creating Private Enterprises and Efficient Markets* (Washington, D.C.: The World Bank, 1994).

10. This section is based on the author's experience as project manager for mass privatization in Moldova, and also draws on Ceslav Ciobanu, "Mass Privatization: Case Study of Moldova" (presentation at the training workshop "Mass Privatization: Techniques for Rapid Economic Transformation and Capital Market Development," Institute for Public–Private Partnerships, Washington, D.C., February 15, 1996).

11. John Thornhill, "Moldova Striving for Stability on All Fronts: Small Central European Country is Seen as a Model of Post-Communist Reform," *Financial Times*, London, October 13, 1995, 10.

CHAPTER SEVEN

PRIVATIZATION AND CAPITAL MARKETS

Looking to the Future

This chapter discusses the interaction of privatization and capital market development for sectors which are becoming increasingly important for current and future economic growth: the provision of economic infrastructure (especially telecommunications and power) and institutional investors (especially social security and pension funds).

The decision by governments in developing countries in the 1950s and 1960s to intervene in areas of economic infrastructure such as telecommunications and power was unfortunate for two reasons. Intervention has created inefficient, poorly managed utilities that hinder growth. It has also denied capital markets the chance to develop and eventually meet the financial needs of these enterprises. Deprived of a logical market for their services, capital markets, if they exist at all, tend to be "thin" and to fall short in transforming saving into productive investment.

The privatization of institutional investors, such as pension funds, insurance companies, and mutual funds, is vital for creating demand for capital markets instruments such as stocks and bonds, and for promoting their professional management.

ECONOMIC INFRASTRUCTURE

There is an enormous, ongoing demand for economic infrastructure in the power, telecommunications, transportation, water, and municipal services sectors. To meet this demand, Latin America will have to invest an estimated $60 billion per year, and Asia at least $200 billion a year, until the year 2000.[1] To ease the infrastructure financing crunch, countries have opened these sectors to private participation under such arrangements as public, broad-based sale of shares (discussed in Chapter 5) and Build–Operate–Transfer arrangements. These undertakings both draw upon and encourage strong domestic capital markets and provide a market for foreign investment.

A BOT project is sponsored by a contractor, equipment supplier, and other owners who, under agreement with government, build and operate the required infrastructure for a contractually specified number of years. At the end of the period, the infrastructure project (e.g., a power plant, bridge, highway) is turned over to the government. Under the Build–Own–Operate variant, the private sector owns the infrastructure project in perpetuity. Other variants are possible.

The BOT project makes money by selling output, such as electricity for the national grid, or by levying fees, such as tolls for bridges or highways. BOT projects must be commercially viable so lenders can be repaid from project revenues and investors can earn an acceptable rate of return. In such a project, a balance of financial interest is required among the project sponsors and owners, project lenders, the host government and the consumers of the infrastructure services. Notable current BOT projects in developing countries include the Taipei Mass Rapid Transit System, the Malaysian North–South Toll Expressway, and the Bangkok Elevated Road and Train System. Table 7.1 identifies leading potential private infrastructure projects.

Financing BOT Infrastructure Projects through Capital Markets

There are three basic financing features of BOT projects which make them draw heavily on capital markets for equity and long-term debt: They tend to involve large sums of money (sometimes more than $1 billion), are highly leveraged (i.e., the project–finance ratio of debt to equity is high), and are of long duration. Debt often represents 70 to 90 percent of project finance. The debt portion requires long maturities, often ten to fifteen years, corresponding to the economic life and payback period of the projects. BOT projects will draw on the main components of the financial markets, and will require that each be relatively developed and competitive: the equity market, the banks, and possibly the bond market.

BOT projects quickly uncover any inadequacies of domestic capital markets. Since the domestic capital markets in most developing countries are still in the early stages of development, domestic finance is inadequate for most large BOT projects. These BOT projects must seek foreign investment as a part of the financing package.

BOT projects thrive on the complementarity between equity markets and the banking sector. A successful BOT project is one that is bankable: Debt financing can be raised to complement owners' equity. This creates a sound financial base to see the project through to completion and operation. Institutional investors will play a critical role in raising the required finance.

At present, BOT projects rely largely on the non-securitized capital markets, such as privately placed equity and bank loans. Yet stock and bond markets are also needed. BOT projects in some of the more dynamic emerging markets, such as Thailand and Malaysia, have raised finance by selling stocks and bonds locally. Clearly, privatization of existing SOEs and of institutional investors can boost

Table 7.1
Top Ten Potential Private Infrastructure Projects (September 1995)

Location	Project	Contract	Cost (US$ millions)
Russia	National long-distance telephone network	BO license	40,000
Belarus/Germany/Poland/Russia	Yamal gas pipeline	BOO	39,700
Hong Kong	Chek Lap Kok airport	BLO	20,000
Russia	RAO Gazprom	Privatization, 60%	20,000
Taiwan (China)	Taipei-Kaohsiung high-speed rail	BOT, 30 years	17,400
India	West Bengal coal-fired power plants	BOT	12,700
Germany	Deutsche Bundespost Telekom	Privatization, 25%	9,750
United Kingdom	Railtrack	Privatization	9,500
China/Hong Kong	Beijing-Hong Kong highway	BOT	8,000
Taiwan (China)	Kaohsiung rapid transit system	Privatization	7,600

Source: "The Private Infrastructure Industry—A Global Market of US$60 Billion a Year," a report prepared by the Private Sector Development Department, World Bank, Washington, D.C., 1995.

Note: BO = Build–Operate; BLO = Build–Lease–Operate; BOO = Build–Own–Operate; BOT = Build–Operate–Transfer.

infrastructure financing by stimulating equity and bond markets.

The success of the British and French privatization programs doubtless helped to convince policymakers and the private sector to construct the Channel Tunnel, which cost about $19 billion, on a private sector BOT basis. Although this project has not been without its problems—no project of this size and technical and financial complexity could expect to go perfectly—the risks and costs have been borne by the private sector, in the absence of which the project would not have been started.

Telecommunications and power are two of the leading infrastructure sectors, and are critical to economic growth. The main privatization options include public share sales and BOT arrangements.

Telecommunications

The poor provision of telecommunications services by government in developing and developed countries, the large levels of finance needed for investment, rapid advances in technology, and the possibilities for significant cost reductions through competition make it imperative for governments to wrench loose telecommunications from the SOE bureaucracy and turn it over to the private sector.

Many of the largest and best-known privatizations have been of telephone companies. In developed economies, these include the United Kingdom's British Telecom, Japan's NTT, Danish Tele Danmark, and the Dutch KPN. Privatization proceeds from telecommunication companies for the remainder of the 1990s has been estimated at about $100 billion worldwide, including the planned privatization of Germany's huge Deutsche Telekom in 1996.[2]

In Latin America and Asia, even though policies to unbundle monopoly elements of telephone companies and foster competition have been less than perfect, the privatization of telephone companies has improved services for customers, increased the growth of direct exchange lines, and improved management. Privatization in the telecommunications sectors has increased activity in local stock markets. Investors have seen total returns on their share investments increase significantly. The challenges these countries still face are to create more competition, especially for long-distance calls, and to regulate, where necessary, in a way that is fair to consumers and investors.

Although most privatizations in the telecommunications sector have taken place through the sale of shares, the sector also lends itself to privatization by the BOT approach. Thailand awarded a concession to a local Thai company, which worked with British Telecom and other foreign advisors to install 2 million lines in Bangkok and another 1 million lines outside of Bangkok. The BOT company will install and operate the lines. Revenue will be divided between the BOT company and the government-owned telephone company.

The largest project to consider using public–private partnerships is Russia's "50x50" telecommunications project, estimated to cost $40 billion. The telecommunications sector in Russia urgently needs to be modernized. As with many developing countries, it suffers from inadequate capacity, low penetration and call-completion rates, and a lack of modern communications services. The national telephone penetration rate is about sixteen lines per 100 people. In the 50x50 infrastructure project, the Russian government intends to modernize the national telecommunications network by installing fifty digital switches throughout various regions of Russia, which will be connected by 50,000 kilometers of fiber optic cable and microwave equipment.[3]

Power

The failure of state-owned electricity companies to keep up with the growth in power demand causes serious problems for many economies. For example, in the Philippines, the state-owned National Power Corporation was unable to meet the surging demand for power. In 1990, power outages in the capital region of Manila alone cost an estimated $2.4 billion in lost economic output. In 1992 and 1993, power was not available for up to seven hours a day.[4] Faced with daunting demand and inadequate resources, governments (and donors) are finding it necessary to open power generation, transmission, and distribution to private firms, whose role in the power sector continues to grow.

Privatization by share sale in the power sector has not reached the same level as in telecommunications, although there are examples in the United Kingdom, Korea, and Malaysia. BOT seems to be the preferred method of privatization in developing countries. Under this approach, a private sector group finances, builds, and operates a power plant for a contractually determined length of time, and generates and sells electricity to the national grid under a power-purchase agreement. One advantage of this method is its stimulation of competition among BOT private sector groups to generate energy at low cost.

Large BOT power projects are currently operational in the People's Republic of China and the Philippines. In Pakistan, the $1.2 billion Hab River oil-fired power plant, a BOT operation, broke ground after seven years of delay. Many other countries are considering using the BOT approach in the power sector.

INSTITUTIONAL INVESTORS

Institutional investors dominate the secondary capital markets in the United States and the United Kingdom. In the primary markets, companies trying to raise capital turn to these large pools of funds.

It makes sense for pension funds and life insurance companies to buy stocks and bonds. These securities enable them to match their long-term liabilities with a portfolio of diversified, high-yielding, long-term assets. Pension funds and life insurance companies are effective at reaching individuals, thus creating a larger pool of savings in the country.

Institutional investors in emerging-market countries (and many developed countries) are usually unable to fulfill their natural role of mobilizing savings for productive economic uses as a consequence of adverse government policies, including the following:

- Government ownership of institutional investors, such as insurance companies and pension funds.
- Unfunded (pay-as-you-go) government-managed social security systems which fail to make use of capital markets.
- Policies which restrict investments to predominantly government bonds that pay low interest rates. Governments do this to help finance the deficit at low cost.

In Sri Lanka, for example, the largest pension funds in the country are the Employees Provident Fund (EPF) and the Employees Trust Fund (ETF). These are basically captive instruments of government. Although technically these funds could diversify the assets they hold, both are subject to directives from the Ministry of Finance which determine investment policy. Both EPF and ETF invest all their funds in either treasury bills or government-owned corporations. It is estimated that in the early 1990s, the EPF funded 60 percent of the government deficit. Both funds earn a negative real return on their investments. This will place the government in a precarious financial position when it comes time to make good on pension promises. It also hinders the development of a more vibrant capital market.

In developing countries, the development of local institutional investors, such as mutual funds, life and other insurance companies, and social security and pension funds is critical for long-term capital market development. Because of their size and the volume of funds involved, institutional investors provide sophisticated demand for capital market instruments. They are a source of finance for new issues, and of stability and sound management for secondary market trading. Professional standards, business considerations, and regulations encourage them to be prudent.

Mutual Funds and Insurance Companies

Mutual funds (also called investment funds) provide an attractive vehicle for financial saving for less affluent households, by providing for diversification of investments across a number of companies and industries, professional management, and low transaction costs. Mutual funds are also used in countries with mass priva-tization programs. These funds collect and pool vouchers and bid on shares in enterprises on behalf of individuals. They have played critical roles in promoting public awareness in mass privatization programs by stimulating the public's demand and interest and explaining some of the basics of capital markets. Once the mass privatization program is completed, investment funds are in a position to become mutual funds for equities and, somewhat later, bonds.

The reserves of life insurance and annuities policies are large and of a long-term nature. They are suitable for investing in corporate equities and bonds. In 1994, priva-tization of insurance companies worldwide amounted to $7.5 billion.

Social Security Funds

In most countries, governments manage social security (public pension) systems. Private pension plans, tied to an employer, also exist and are usually regulated. But social security itself can be privatized, with advantages for retirees, government finance, and capital market development. Regulations affecting private pension plans can be liberalized in many countries to permit investment in equities and corporate bonds. The rest of this discussion will consider social security alone. References to pension plans will assume that they are the plans that result from the privatization of social security.

Virtually all countries need to make fundamental changes in the structure and financing of their social security systems, which face serious difficulties. The United States and Europe face growing demographic pressures that will lead to financial crisis of their social security systems early in the twenty-first century.

In the "pay-as-you-go" social security systems, workers' contributions are paid directly to pensioners. Aging of the population, related to declining birth rates and greater longevity, places increasing strain on pay-as-you-go systems, as workers and employers become increasingly burdened by social security contributions. These demographic trends have forced public social security systems into financial crisis and even insolvency. Most pay-as-you-go systems provide neither a secure retirement, nor a source of investment funds. Pay-as-you-go systems, in addition to being unfunded, are also defined benefit plans. In defined benefit plans, members are paid a pension related to career earnings, such as a predetermined percentage of final or average salary, subject to years of service. This places a significant burden on the government to meet these defined benefits as the population retires.

Given all of the uncertainty about the future performance of the economy, as measured by growth rate, inflation, interest rates, political stability, and other variables, it is difficult in the mature, developed economies to guarantee contractually defined benefits on a long-term basis. In developing countries, given the additional levels of risk, it is especially difficult to guarantee benefits. Under pay-as-you-go systems, people assume that the government will take care of them in old age. Financial and economic awareness and stewardship by the populace over politicians may suffer as a result.

As the World Bank notes, the social security systems of developing countries are particularly fragile. It notes that government pensions are rarely fully indexed to inflation, so workers are poorly protected in their old age.[5] Latin America, Eastern Europe, and the former Soviet Union face immediate problems with their social security systems, which are in need of fundamental reform. Vittas and Michelitsch recommend that these countries move to a system of nonemployer, defined contribution plans based on individual capitalization accounts with full immediate vesting, full portability, and full funding.[6]

The importance of privatizing social security is starting to be appreciated more fully. Social security contributions constitute huge pools of funds that are potentially available for productive investment. A privatized social security system, in which individuals manage their own pension funds, spares the government the fiscal crises inherent in pay-as-you-go systems, while actually providing higher returns and a more secure retirement for pensioners (see Table 7.2).

In defined contribution plans, in contrast to defined benefit plans, contributions are fixed and benefits vary with market returns. The risks are borne, and returns enjoyed, by the employees. Private defined contribution pensions (which by definition are funded), in contrast to public pay-as-you-go social security programs, rely on the performance of a portfolio of investments purchased with the contributions of employees (and usually employers) over the time the individual is in the labor force.

Defined contribution pension plans relieve the government (or employer) of this risk, while enabling the individual to maximize the returns to his or her own retirement fund. Given the long-run nature of this system, equities will be an extremely attractive savings vehicle for such retirement. The use of defined contribution pension plans will also encourage individuals to utilize professionally managed mutual funds, which further contributes to capital market development. It will also give citizens a vested interest in economic reform and sound policy: Economic growth ultimately results in larger dividends and capital gains for shareholders.

Chile: A Model for Privatizing Social Security

Chile successfully privatized its social security system in 1981, when it introduced a government-mandated and -regulated, but privately managed system.[7] This replaced an insolvent social security system that had operated on a pay-as-you-go basis.

The Chilean system is a defined contribution system based on individual capitalization accounts, in which pension

Table 7.2
Average Annual Investment Returns for Selected Pension Funds (1980s)

	Country	Percentage of rate of return after inflation	Years
Publicly	Peru	-37.4	1981–1988
	Turkey	-23.8	1984–1988
	Zambia	-23.4	1980–1988
Managed	Venezuela	-15.3	1980–1989
	Egypt	-11.7	1981–1989
	Ecuador	-10.0	1980–1986
	Kenya	-3.8	1980–1990
	India	0.3	1980–1990
	Singapore	3.0	1980–1990
	Malaysia	4.6	1980–1990
	U.S. OASI[a]	4.8	1980–1990
Privately	Netherlands (occupational)	6.7	1980–1990
	US (occupational)	8.0	1980–1990
Managed	UK (occupational)	8.8	1980–1990
	Chile (AFPs)	9.2	1981–1990

Source: World Bank, *Averting the Old Age Crisis* (New York: Oxford University Press, 1994).

[a]Old-Age and Survivor's Insurance.

benefits depend on the contributions made over a person's working career and the investment income earned on accumulated balances. The Chilean system is privately managed by a number of authorized pension-management companies, known as AFPs. Under this system, 10 percent of the worker's paycheck is deposited into an individual savings account managed by a private fund of the worker's choosing. The government's only role is to regulate the funds and ensure a minimum pension in case the pension received from the privatized funds falls below a subsistence level.

Chile's labor force has responded well to the new system: More than 80 percent of workers have opted for the private systems and contribute to the pension funds. Although some citizens were initially hesitant to join, the private funds realized average real returns of 9.2 percent a year, substantially higher than any other social security system worldwide (see Table 7.2).

In 1992, Chile's total pension pool was estimated at $7 billion, or 25 percent of the country's GDP.[8] By 1995, the pension pool was over $19.2 billion, "enough to give Chile a savings rate approaching that of some Asian nations."[9] This pool of contributions, now representing about 35 percent of Chile's gross domestic product, has served as the foundation for a vibrant capital market consisting of stocks, bonds, and other financial instruments. Argentina, Venezuela, and Columbia have adopted variations on Chile's privatization of its social security system.

BENEFITS OF PRIVATIZING INSTITUTIONAL INVESTORS FOR CAPITAL MARKETS

The privatization of institutional investors, especially social security, offers an excellent means to develop capital markets. At least five benefits of privatizing institutional investors can be identified: increase in the demand for equities and bonds, new sources of investment capital, more efficient and stable capital markets, greater market liquidity, and corporate governance.[10]

Increased Demand for Equities and Bonds

Pension funds have a long-term outlook and are concerned with real returns over time. They also have a predictable inflow of funds, and their time horizon allows them to focus on long-term assets. It makes sense that pensions funds are attracted to equities, which historically have high rates of returns.

Corporate bonds are also attractive to pension, and especially insurance, funds, because interest payments and repayment of original principal are predictable. Thus, pension funds are a natural catalyst for the development of corporate bond markets. The emergence of the corporate bond market will complement the growing equity markets and lead to more complete financial markets.

New Sources of Investment Capital

Private sector pension funds, mutual funds, and insurance companies create pools of medium- and long-term domestic finance for domestic investment. This domestication of finance, in turn, lowers the need for (occasionally controversial) foreign investment.

Private pension funds are an attractive source of funds for emerging economies, especially the former command economies, which need capital for restructuring, new technology, and new markets. These funds can play a significant role in the financing, on a private sector basis, of economic infrastructure projects. The long-term investment objectives of pension funds match the long-term horizon and financing needs of such projects. Through their participation, private pension funds attract other investors to spread the risks and benefits. Private pension funds can also be a source of purchasing power for privatization of SOEs. In Chile, for example, the pension funds have purchased shares in privatized state-owned companies.

More Efficient and Stable Capital Markets

Private institutional investors contribute to the more efficient allocation of capital among enterprises through encouraging better quality information used for making investment decisions. In working with brokers and dealers, institutional investors encourage the development of fundamental research capabilities for the economy, the stock market, industries, and individual companies. Trained professional analysts and portfolio managers monitor companies, industries, and the economy. They demand better information from enterprises to help identify and separate good companies from poor performers. Company and industry risk can be better identified and quantified, and therefore more efficiently priced. The need for high quality information can promote the adoption of modern, internationally accepted accounting and auditing standards.

Pension funds manage large sums of capital and can act as a stabilizing force in cases of market volatility. Given the potential scale of resources managed by institutional investors, they can influence the overall efficiency of financial intermediation in an economy.

Greater Market Liquidity

A key requirement of pension funds and other institutional investors is liquidity; that is, the ability to trade in large amounts without large price swings, and at low transaction cost. Liquidity may be aided by reduction in commissions, which large pension plans can negotiate. Increases in liquidity, in turn, should be beneficial to the efficiency of capital markets and reduce the cost of capital. Private institutional investors also tend to promote improved trading and clearing and settlement systems, and are a force for computerization of the capital markets infrastructure. Improved infrastructure, in turn, improves market liquidity.

Corporate Governance

Governance of private companies is improved by responding to active shareholders representing large blocks of company shares. In countries whose pension funds tend to invest more heavily in equities, the funds can play a potentially influential role in corporate governance. Although pension funds have historically been passive, recent trends indicate greater activism.

The implications of inefficient SOEs and distorted financial markets for governments are straightforward. Policy dialogue must be stepped up to explain to governments why the failure to privatize reduces the efficiency, productivity, and growth of the economy and hinders the development of more efficient capital markets, which further constrains economic growth. Privatization needs to expand in scope and increase in intensity.

Governments must also take steps to support capital market development. Public-awareness programs are needed to explain the benefits of capital markets and privatization. A regulatory framework is necessary for the public to have confidence in capital market instruments. Governments must become aware of the synergies between capital market development and privatization so that both programs will benefit. Privatizing the process of privatization will enable capital markets infrastructure and agents to develop.

The type of privatization chosen will have important implications for developing capital markets. Two of the most significant forms of privatization are also among the best for promoting capital markets. Governments must transfer remaining SOEs to the private sector using the combined techniques of broad-based share sales of the best, blue-chip SOEs, and mass privatization by vouchers for the remaining medium and large enterprises.

These two techniques are also politically astute. Broad-based share sales and mass privatization by vouchers have the particular advantage of making the population a part of the newly emerging capital markets immediately. Economic adjustment, whether in the United Kingdom, Jamaica, or Moldova, involves some difficult changes for the population. Making citizens shareholders, however, enables them to share in the benefits of reform. Broad-based equity ownership encourages the population to use the services of institutional investors, such as mutual funds, insurance companies, and private sector pension funds.

Additional areas of the economy, especially economic infrastructure (telecommunications, power, transportation, and municipal services), must be opened to the private sector through BOT and related techniques. The privatization of potential institutional investors, including social security, must be pursued. With the drive to privatize and develop capital markets, significant sums of money will flow to the now privatized pension funds. The pension funds will become a force in the secondary markets, providing professionalism and stability. In addition, these funds will provide a source of finance to be tapped by private sector companies wishing to sell their shares on the market. The development of large pools of investment funds managed by private sector institutional investors allows large infrastructure projects to be increasingly financed from domestic sources.

The effort to expand the scope of privatization will increase the breadth, depth and efficiency of capital markets. The parallel streams and cross-cutting currents of privatization and capital market development will contribute to overall economic growth.

Privatization and capital markets development should be among the easier planks of economic reform for governments to implement. Privatizations can be structured to provide benefits to virtually all citizens. Workers and managers of SOEs can also benefit through preferential access to shares. Governments which privatize successfully tend to fare well politically, as citizens realize that economic reform promotes growth and higher incomes. Privatization and capital market development will not solve all problems by themselves, but they are required steps on the road to growth and development.

BIBLIOGRAPHY

Adam, Christopher, William Cavendish, and Percy S. Mistry.
   *Adjusting Privatization: Case Studies from Developing
   Countries*. London: James Currey Ltd., 1992.
Ambrose, William W., Paul R. Hennemeyer, and Jean-Paul
   Chapon. "Privatizing Telecommunications Systems." IFC
   discussion paper no. 10, The World Bank, Washington, D.C.,
   1990.
The Aries Group. "A Study of Securities Market Institutions:
   Philippines." Report prepared for the Asian Develop-
   ment Bank, Washington, D.C., 1990.
———. "A Study of Securities Market Institutions: Sri Lanka."
   Report prepared for the Asian Development Bank, Wash-
   ington, D.C., 1990.
———. "A Study of Securities Market Institutions: Thailand."
   Report prepared for the Asian Development Bank, Washington, D.C., 1990.
Arthur Young, Inc. "Central American Capital Markets." Re-
   port prepared for the Agency for International Develop-
   ment, Regional Office for Central America and Panama,
   Washington, D.C., October 1987.
———. "Financing Privatization Under Limited Capital Conditions." Report prepared for the U.S. Agency for International Development, Washington, D.C., November 1986.

Augenblick, Mark, and B. Scott Custer, Jr. "The Build, Oper-
    ate, and Transfer ("BOT") Approach to Infrastructure
    Projects in Developing Countries." The World Bank,
    Working paper WPS 498, Washington, D.C., 1990.
Basak, Zafer Z. "Teletas: A Turkish Privatization Case Study."
    Report prepared for the Center for Privatization, Wash-
    ington D.C., 1988.
Bell, Stuart W. "Sharing the Wealth: Privatization through
    Broad-Based Ownership Strategies." Discussion paper
    No. 285, The World Bank, Washington, D.C., April 1995.
Berg, Elliot, and Mary Shirley. "Divestiture in Developing
    Countries." Discussion paper 11, The World Bank, Wash-
    ington, D.C., 1987.
Bishop, Robert M. "Improving Colombo Stock Exchange Regu-
    lation." Report prepared for the U.S. Agency for Interna-
    tional Development, Colombo, Sri Lanka, 1990.
Borensztein, Eduardo, and Manmohan S. Kumar. "Proposals
    for Privatization in Eastern Europe." IFC Staff Papers,
    Vol. 38, No. 2, International Monetary Fund, Washington,
    D.C., 1991.
Boycko, Maxim, Andrei Shleifer, and Robert Vishny. Privatizing
    Russia. Cambridge, Mass.: MIT Press, 1995.
Brainard, Lawrence J. "Reform in Eastern Europe: Creating a
    Capital Market." Federal Reserve Bank of Kansas City
    Economic Review 76 (January/February 1991).
Chrisney, Martin D. "Financing Trends for Private Infrastruc-
    ture in Latin America and The Caribbean." The Finan-
    cier: Analyses of Capital and Money Market Transactions.
    3 (February, 1996).
Chuppe, Terry. "Regulation of Capital Markets in Emerging
    Market Countries." Presentation at the training workshop,
    "Mass Privatization: Techniques for Rapid Economic
    Transformation and Capital Market Development," Insti-
    tute for Public–Private Partnerships, Washington, D.C.,
    21 February 1996.
Ciobanu, Ceslav. "Mass Privatization: Case Study of Moldova."
    Presentation at the training workshop, "Mass Privatization:
    Techniques for Rapid Economic Transformation and Capi-
    tal Market Development," Institute for Public–Private Part-
    nerships, Washington, D.C., 16 February 1996.
Cook, Paul, and Colin Kirkpatrick, eds. Privatisation in Less
    Developed Countries. New York: St. Martin's Press, 1988.

Columbia Journal of World Business, Focus Issue: Privatization 28 (Spring 1993).

Cowan, L. Gray. *Privatization in the Developing World*. Westport, Conn.: Greenwood Press, 1990.

Debs, Richard A., David L. Roberts, and Eli M. Remolona. *Finance for Developing Countries*. New York and London: Group of Thirty, 1987.

Demirguc-Kunt, Asli, and Vojislav Maksimovic. "Stock Market Development and Firm Financing Choices." Policy research working paper 1461, The World Bank, Washington, D.C., 1995.

Dhanji, Farid and Branko Milanovic. "Privatization in Eastern and Central Europe," World Bank Working Paper, WPS 770, Washington, D.C., 1992.

Donahue, John D. *The Privatization Decision: Public Ends, Private Means*. New York: Basic Books, 1989.

Elicker, Paul. "Privatization in Eastern Europe: What the Potential Foreign Investor Needs to Know." *Business Economics* 25 (October 1990).

El-Naggar, Said, ed. *Privatization and Structural Adjustment in the Arab Countries*. Washington, D.C.: International Monetary Fund, 1989.

Ernst and Young. *Privatization: Investing in State-Owned Enterprises around the World*. New York: John Wiley & Sons, 1994.

Ferrara, Peter. "The Privatization of Social Security in Chile." *Journal of Economic Growth* 3 (Spring 1989).

Galal, Ahmed, and Mary Shirley, eds. *Does Privatization Deliver? Highlights from a World Bank Conference*. Washington, D.C.: The World Bank, 1994.

Gill, David. "Privatization and Internationalization of Securities Markets: Opportunities for Financial Market Development." International Finance Corporation, Washington, D.C. Mimeographed.

———. "Two Decades of Change in Emerging Markets." In *The World's Emerging Stock Markets*, edited by Keith K.H. Park and Antoine van Agtmael. Chicago: Probus, 1992.

Guerard, Yves, and Glenn Jenkins. *Building Private Pension Systems: A Handbook*. San Francisco: ICS Press, 1993.

Hanke, Steve H., ed. *Privatization and Development*. San Francisco: Institute for Contemporary Studies, 1987.

Hanke, Steve H., and Alan A. Walters, eds. *Capital Markets and Development*. San Francisco: Institute for Contemporary Studies, 1991.

Hensley, Matthew L. "An Assessment of the Malaysian Privatization Program: Innovative Responses to Global Competition." Report prepared for U.S. Trade and Development Agency, Washington D.C., 1992.

———. "Integrating Infrastructure Privatization into a Mass Privatization Program." Presentation at the training workshop, "Mass Privatization: Techniques for Rapid Economic Transformation and Capital Market Development," Institute for Public–Private Partnerships, Washington, D.C., 13 February 1996.

Hensley, Matthew L., and Edward White. "The Privatization Experience in Malaysia." *Columbia Journal of World Business* 28 (Spring 1993).

Holden, Paul, and Sarath Rajapatirana. *Unshackling the Private Sector: A Latin American Story.* Washington, D.C.: The World Bank, 1995.

International Finance Corporation. *Emerging Stock Markets Factbook.* Washington, D.C.: The International Finance Corporation, various years.

———. "Financing Corporate Growth in the Developing World." IFC discussion paper no. 12, The World Bank, Washington, D.C., 1991.

———. *Privatization: Principles and Practice.* Washington, D.C.: The World Bank, 1995.

International Monetary Fund. *International Capital Markets: Developments, Prospects and Policy Issues.* Washington, D.C.: The International Monetary Fund, 1995.

"Interview with Pedro-Pablo Kuczynski." *Columbia Journal of World Business* 26 (Summer 1991).

Jayasinghe, Tissa. "Publicizing Privatization: Sri Lanka's Public Awareness Program." Paper presented at the International Privatization: Global Trends, Policies, Processes and Experiences Conference, Saskatoon, Saskatchewan, May 1990.

Jenkins, Glenn. Supplement to *Public Finances/Finances Publiques.* 47 (1992): 141-151.

Joslin, William. "The Mass Privatization Alternative." Presentation at the training workshop, "Mass Privatization: Techniques for Rapid Economic Transformation and Capital Market Development," Institute for Public–Private Partnerships, Washington, D.C., 13 February 1996.

Kassahun, Yohannes. "Legal Aspects of Mass Privatization and Capital Market Development." Presentation at the training workshop, "Mass Privatization: Techniques for Rapid Economic Transformation and Capital Market Development," Institute for Public–Private Partnerships, Washington, D.C., 19 February 1996.

Kaufman, Henry. *Interest Rates, the Markets, and the New Financial World*. New York: Times Books, 1986.

Kikeri, Sunita, John Nellis, and Mary Shirley. *Privatization: The Lessons of Experience*. Washington, D.C.: The World Bank, 1992.

Koika, Gabriela. "Techniques for Mass Privatization." Presentation at the training workshop, "Mass Privatization: Techniques for Rapid Economic Transformation and Capital Market Development," Institute for Public–Private Partnerships, Washington, D.C., 14–15 February 1996.

Leeds Roger S. "Malaysia: Genesis of a Privatization Transaction." *World Development* 17, no. 5 (1989).

———. "Privatization in Jamaica: Two Case Studies." Cambridge, Mass.: Paper prepared for the Harvard University Center for Business and Government, 1987.

———. "Turkey: Rhetoric and Reality." In *The Promise of Privatization*, edited by Raymond Vernon. New York: The Council on Foreign Relations, 1988.

Leeds, Roger S., and Michael Harman. "Securities Market Development and Privatization." In *Russia: Creating Private Enterprises and Efficient Markets*, edited by Ira W. Lieberman and John Nellis. Washington, D.C.: The World Bank, 1994.

Letwin, Oliver. *Privatising the World*. London: Cassell, 1988.

Levine, Ross and Sara Zervos. "Policy, Stock Market Development and Long-Run Growth." Paper presented at a World Bank Conference, Washington, D.C., February 1995.

Lieberman, Ira W., Andrew Ewing, Michal Mejstrik, Joyita Mukherjee, and Peter Fidler, eds. *Mass Privatization In Central and Eastern Europe and the Former Soviet Union: A Comparative Analysis*. Washington, D.C.: The World Bank, 1995.

Lieberman, Ira W., and John Nellis, eds. *Russia: Creating Private Enterprises and Efficient Markets*. Washington, D.C.: The World Bank, 1994.

Ludvik, Carl W., and Ronald J. Ivey. "A Case Study of the Honduras Privatization Program." Paper prepared for the Center for Privatization, Washington, D.C., December 1989.

The MAC Group. "Capital Markets and Privatization." Report prepared for the U.S. Agency for International Development, Washington, D.C., 1987.

Mako, William. "Strategies for Mass Privatization." Presentation at the training workshop, "Mass Privatization: Techniques for Rapid Economic Transformation and Capital Market Development," Institute for Public–Private Partnerships, Washington, D.C., 14 February 1996.

Marquardt, Alexander, and Ellen H. Clark. "French Privatizations and International Capital Markets." *Northwestern Journal of International Law & Business* 15 (1994): 408.

McGreevey, William. "Social Security in Latin America: Issues and Options for the World Bank." Discussion paper, No. 110, The World Bank, Washington, D.C., 1990.

McLindon, Michael P. "Advantages of Privatizing Social Security." Presentation at the training workshop, "Public–Private Partnerships in Social Infrastructure," Institute for Public–Private Partnerships, Washington, D.C., 30 October 1995.

———. "BOT Infrastructure Privatization." Presentation to the Asian Development Bank, Manilla, Philippines, 1992 and 1993.

———. "Capital and Securities Markets." Presentation at the "Enterprise and Investment Lawyers Course," International Development Law Institute, Rome, Italy, 21–23 June 1995.

———. "Debt-Equity Swaps: Partial Solution to the Debt Crisis?" Paper presented at the International Roundtable, National Association of Business Economists, Washington, D.C., 27 February 1989.

———. "Linking Mass Privatization and Capital Markets." Presentation at the training workshop, "Mass Privatization: Techniques for Rapid Economic Transformation and Capital Market Development," Institute for Public–Private Partnerships, Washington, D.C., 19 February 1996.

———. "Macroeconomic Aspects of Privatization: The Case of Jamaica." Paper presented at the Seminar on Privatization Strategies and Techniques for Development, Center for Privatization, Washington, D.C., 1988.

———. "New Sources of Financing for Infrastructure Projects." Presentation at the training workshop, "Infrastructure Investment and Financial Analysis," Institute for Public–Private Partnerships, Washington, D.C., 30 August 1995.

————. "Privatization and Securities Markets in Developing Countries." Training workshop presentation and paper presented to the World Bank, Washington, D.C., 30 June 1992.

————. "Privatization by Sale of Shares and BOT Techniques." Presentation at the "Enterprise and Investment Lawyers Course," International Development Law Institute, Rome, Italy, June 1993.

————. Review of *Small Island Economies,* by DeLisle Worrell. *Business Economics* 24 (July 1989): 67–68.

————. "Utilities and Monopolies: Unbundling, Market Structure and Privatization." Presentation at the training workshop, "Regulation of Utilities and Monopolies," Institute for Public–Private Partnerships, Washington, D.C., 5 December 1995.

McLindon, Michael P., and Richard B. Samuelson. "Korea 1992: Foreign Perspective." *Business Korea* (July 1990).

————. "One More Push: Sri Lanka's Bourse is Ripe for More Reform." *Far Eastern Economic Review,* 155 (February 13 1992).

————. "Privatization and Capital Markets in Developing Countries." Paper presented to the World Bank, Washington, D.C., 28 January 1991.

————. "Selling Thailand Inc." *Far Eastern Economic Review,* 152 (June 20 1991).

McLindon, Michael P., Richard Downer, Richard Samuelson, David Levintow, and David Smith. "Privatization in Thailand." Report prepared for the Center for Privatization, Washington, D.C., 1990.

McLindon, Michael P., Richard Samuelson, Marianne Page, and Niall Shiner. "Sri Lanka." In *The World's Emerging Stock Markets,* edited by Keith K. H. Park and Antoine van Agtmael. Chicago: Probus 1992.

Megginson, William L., Robert C. Nash, and Matthias van Randenborgh. "The Privatization Dividend: A Worldwide Analysis of the Financial and Operating Performance of Newly Privatized Firms." *Public Policy for the Private Sector,* Washington, D.C., The World Bank Group, December 1995.

Mobius, Mark. *The Investors' Guide to Emerging Markets.* New York: Irwin Professional Publishing, 1995.

Nankani, Helen. *Selected Country Case Studies.* Vol. 2 of *Techniques of Privatization of State-Owned Enterprises.* Washington, D.C.: The World Bank, 1988.

Odle, Maurice. "Foreign Direct Investment as Part of the Privatization Process." *Transnational Corporations* 2 (August 1993).

Organization for Economic Co-operation and Development (OECD). *Financial Market Trends*. Paris: OECD, 1995.

———. *Mass Privatization: An Initial Assessment*. Paris: OECD, 1995.

Pardy, Robert. "Institutional Reform in Emerging Securities Markets." Working paper WPS 907, The World Bank, Washington, D.C., 1992.

———. "Regulatory and Institutional Impacts of Securities Market Computerization." Working paper WPS 866, The World Bank, Washington, D.C., 1992.

Pinkham, Richard. "The Privatization of Port Kelang." Presentation at the training workshop, "Implementing BOO and BOT Projects," the Institute for Public–Private Partnerships, Washington, D.C., 18 March 1996.

Porter, Michael E. *The Competitive Advantage of Nations*. New York: The Free Press, 1990.

"Privatisation: Everybody's Doing It, Differently." *The Economist*, 21 December 1985.

Privatisation International. *Privatisation Yearbook 1995*. London: Privatisation International, 1995.

Reason Foundation. *Privatization 1995*. Los Angeles, Calif.: The Reason Foundation, 1995.

Redwood, John. "The Democratic Revolutions: Popular Capitalism in Eastern Europe." Policy study, Center for Policy Studies, London, 1990.

———. "Equity for Everyman." Policy study, Center for Policy Studies, London, 1986.

———. *Popular Capitalism*. London: Routledge, 1988.

———. "Privatization: A Consultant's Perspective." In *Privatization and Deregulation in Global Perspective,* edited by Dennis J. Gayle and Jonathan N. Goodrich. New York: Quorum Books, 1989.

Roth, Gabriel. *The Private Provision of Public Services*. New York: Oxford University Press, 1987.

Sachs, Jeffrey. "Helping Russia: Goodwill is Not Enough." *The Economist,* 21 December 1991.

———. *Poland's Jump to the Market Economy*. Cambridge, Mass.: The MIT Press, 1993.

Saghir, Jamal. "Tunisian Privatization Program." Report prepared for Center for Privatization, Washington, D.C., 1990.

Salomon Brothers. "Privatization: A Latin American Success Story." Salomon Brothers, New York, 1992.

Sambunaris, Georgia A. "The Prospects for Multinational Banking in Mexico." Masters Thesis, Georgetown University, Washington, D.C., August 1995.

Samuelson, Richard B. "Prospects for Investing in Korea." *Business Korea* (May 1988).

Savas, E. S. *Privatization: The Key to Better Government.* Chatham, N.J.: Chatham House, 1987.

Segura, Jorge F. "Privatization of State-Owned Enterprises in Honduras." Report prepared for the Center for Privatization, Washington, D.C., 1988.

Shafik, Nemat. "Making a Market: Mass Privatization in the Czech and Slovak Republics." Policy research working paper 1231. The World Bank, Washington, D.C., 1993.

Skogstad, Samuel. "Policy Reform and the Transition from Command to Market Economy: A Conceptual Overview." Paper prepared for the Policy Research Center, Georgia State University, 1995.

Stanley, Marjorie T. *The Irwin Guide to Investing in Emerging Markets.* Chicago: Irwin, 1995.

Sudweeks, Brian L. *Equity Market Development in Developing Countries.* New York: Praeger, 1989.

Toso, Roberto. "The Chilean Privatization Experience." Cambridge, Mass.: Paper prepared for Harvard University, Center for International Affairs, 1990.

Vernon, Raymond, ed. *The Promise of Privatization.* New York: The Council on Foreign Relations, 1988.

Vittas, Dimitri. "Contractual Savings and Emerging Securities Markets." Working paper WPS 858, The World Bank, Washington, D.C., 1992.

Vittas, Dimitri, and Augusto Iglesias. "The Rationale and Performance of Personal Pension Plans in Chile." Working paper WPS 867, The World Bank, Washington, D.C., 1992.

Vittas, Dimitri, and Roland Michelitsch. "Pension Funds in Central Europe and Russia: Their Prospects and Potential Role in Corporate Governance." Policy research working paper 1459, The World Bank, Washington, D.C., 1995.

Vuylsteke, Charles. *Methods and Implementation.* Vol. 1 of *Techniques of Privatization of State-Owned Enterprises.* Washington, D.C.: The World Bank, 1988.

White, Edward. "Financial Structuring of Public–Private Partnerships in Infrastructure." Presentation at the training workshop, "Infrastructure Investment and Financial

Analysis: Successful Techniques for Developing Public
and Private Infrastructure Projects in the 1990s." Institute for Public–Private Partnerships, Washington, D.C.,
26 March 1996.

White, Thomas. "Post-Privatization Enterprise Restructuring."
Presentation at the training workshop, "Mass Privatiza-
tion: Techniques for Rapid Economic Transformation and
Capital Market Development," Institute for Public–Private
Partnerships, Washington, D.C., 19 February 1996.

———. "Understanding the Competitive Market Environment."
Presentation at the training workshop, "Demonopoliza-
tion and Post-Privatization Management," Institute for
Public–Private Partnerships, Washington, D.C., 13 November 1995.

World Bank. *Adjustment in Africa.* New York: Oxford University
Press, 1994.

———. "Argentina: Capital Markets Study." Report prepared by
the World Bank, Washington, D.C., 1994.

———. *Argentina's Privatization Program: Experience, Issues,
and Lessons.* (Washington, D.C.: The World Bank, 1993).

———. *Averting the Old Age Crisis.* New York: Oxford University Press, 1994.

———. *Bureaucrats in Business.* New York: Oxford University
Press, 1995.

———. *The East Asian Miracle.* New York: Oxford University
Press, 1993.

———. *The Emerging Asian Bond Market.* Washington, D.C.:
The World Bank, 1995.

———. *World Development Report.* New York: Oxford University
Press, various years.

World Equity and the International Finance Corporation. *Privatisation in Emerging Markets.* London: World Equity, 1993.

Zank, Neal S., John A. Mathieson, Frank T. Nieder, Kathleen
D. Vickland, and Ronald J. Ivey. *Reforming Financial
Systems: Policy Change and Privatization.* Westport,
Conn.: Greenwood Press, 1991.

INDEX

Accounting: and auditing in SOEs, 14; capital markets and, 5; CFA program and, 70; financial institutions in Sri Lanka and, 106; government intervention and development of, 50; impact of foreign portfolio investors on, 38; impact of private pension funds on, 147; mass privatization and, 113, 118; possibilities for privatization without adequate, 21; stock exchange and, 55

Africa, privatization and economic reform in, 29–31

American Depositary Receipts (ADRs), 5, 12 n. 9, 90, 94, 100

Argentina: number of shareholders in, 82; privatization and capital markets in, 89–91; privatization of economic infrastructure in, 4; privatization and foreign investment in, 37; privatization of social security in, 145; SOEs and foreign debt in, 28; structuring a share sale in, 83

Asia, 4; privatization of economic infrastructure, 134, 137; privatization and economic reform in, 28–29; privatization by share sale and capital markets in, 79, 98–107. *See also under names of specific countries*

Assets, 17, 23, 41–43

Association of Investment Management and Research (AIMR), 70

Auctions: in mass privatization, use of pilot, 128; in Moldova, 127–128; open-outcry, 19, 80; privatization plan and, 118; in Russia, 125; share registry and protocol of voucher, 65–66; tradable vouchers and, 116; unpriced bids and subscription for shares, 19–120. *See also* Mass privatization

"Back-office" operations, 36, 64
Balance sheets, 5, 56, 103, 118
Banks and banking systems, 5, 58 n. 6; and balance sheets,

About the Author

MICHAEL P. McLINDON is the president of Emerging Markets Research and Investments. Dr. McLindon is a privatization and capital markets specialist with many years of experience in the emerging market countries of Asia, Latin America, Africa and Europe. He has published and lectured widely in this area. He is also a Chartered Financial Analyst (CFA).

ISBN 0-275-95066-2

90000>

EAN

9 780275 950668

HARDCOVER BAR CODE